KEEPING YOUR KIDS SAFE

5/5 due

KEEPING YOUR KIDS SAFE

A Handbook For Caring Parents

Gene Brown

MONARCH
PRESS
NEW YORK

KEEPING YOUR KIDS SAFE

Produced by Cloverdale Press
133 Fifth Avenue
New York, New York 10003

Published by Monarch Press
A Division of Simon & Schuster, Inc.
Simon & Schuster Building
Rockefeller Center
1230 Avenue of the Americas
New York, New York 10020
MONARCH PRESS and colophon are registered
trademarks of Simon & Schuster, Inc.

Cover design by David M. Nehila
Typography by *Paragraphics*
Manufactured in the United States of America

1 2 3 4 5 6 7 8 9 10

Library of Congress Catalog Card Number: 84-62846
ISBN: 0-671-60459-7 cloth
      0-671-55621-5 pbk.

CONTENTS

Introduction 1

1. The Very Young 3

2. Teaching Safety 19

3. Make Your Home Safe—All Year Long 33

4. In an Emergency 57

5. When You Can't Be Around 73

6. Vehicular Safety 81

7. The Child Outdoors 91

8. Away from Home 107

9. Muggings, Abduction, and Sexual Abuse 115

Appendix 127

INTRODUCTION

Yes, you *can* keep your children safe!

Most accidents occur because of carelessness or ignorance. You can minimize both by making your home safe and by teaching your kids what to watch out for, indoors and out.

Safety lessons don't have to be a bore. You can make them fun by turning them into a game, as you'll see in the section on the Home Safety Inventory. You can also use your lessons in safety to give your children a warm sense of self-respect, as they realize you're *trusting* them to take care.

Safety itself doesn't have to be a bore! You don't have to stop doing things; you just have to do them in a smart way. In this book, you'll learn the basic safety measures necessary to give your kids a safe but exciting life.

- You'll start by learning how to make your home and backyard safe for the very youngest member of the family. Then, you'll see how to pass on the safety message to your youngster as he or she gets older.

1

- Next, we'll take you and your family on a treasure hunt, as you make a home safety inventory together—and have a lot of fun doing it. And we'll give you the essential first aid information you need to manage a crisis until the doctor comes.

- Then, we'll show you how to apply your safety techniques to the world outside. There's a chapter that shows you how to prepare your child *and* his temporary caretakers for the times when you're not around. And there's another chapter on vehicular safety, covering everything from school buses to bikes.

- Finally, we'll follow your child on her travels—from a trip to the local playground to a voyage across the seas. We'll give you and her a permanent "safety kit" to take wherever she goes. The kit includes precautions for the unthinkable: muggings, abduction, and child abuse. Your child does *not* have to be a helpless victim—but it is up to you to face facts and give her the knowledge and the confidence she needs. In the last chapter, we'll show you how.

No book can fill your child with the love and trust he needs to be able to take your lessons to heart. Only you can give him those—by loving and trusting him, yourself. But we can give you the facts, techniques, and wisdom accumulated from the experience of others who care.

That's what you'll find in this book.

1
THE VERY YOUNG

The very young are not like the rest of us. Their world is one of light and color, sounds, touches, and tastes. They experience all these delectable things with joy and abandon —and with absolutely no caution!

That's where you, the parent, come in. You certainly *don't* want to curtail or in any way diminish your young child's first explorations of the world. But, insofar as you can, you do want to give your child a safe world to explore. Here's how.

First, it may help you to consider four questions posed by a government pamphlet on safety for young children. Answer "true" or "false":

1. If the phone or doorbell rings while you're busy with your baby, a safe place to leave him is on your bed because you will be gone for *just a moment*. (**True or False**)

2. When you're cooking or serving meals, a good play spot for your toddler is the kitchen floor—where you can keep an eye on him. (**True or False**)

3. Toddlers can be left alone in the bathtub or wading pool if you are careful to put in no more than one or two inches of water. (**True or False**)

4. Toddlers will not try to touch the flames in a barbecue or a fireplace because the heat will frighten them away. (**True or False**)

The answer to all these questions is True, right? A baby placed on the center of a bed can't get very far or do much of anything. A toddler underfoot and under observation can't come to harm. It would take a veritable genius—and it would certainly be beyond an infant—to figure out how to drown in less than two inches of water. That's obvious. And sheer instinct would clearly keep any living creature from poking its hand into a fire.

Let's see exactly why the answer to each of the four statements is actually *False*.

1. Your bed is *not* a safe place for your baby. Unlike audio and video tapes, babies can't be put on "pause," nor can they be put on "hold" like a business associate or a customer on the phone. The rule of thumb is useful here. It holds that if you're far enough away so that you can't lay your thumb flat on your baby's back, you're too far away. Nothing was ever gained by underestimating the power of a baby to roll, squirm, wiggle, and, eventually, in a relatively brief amount of time, slide off a bed. It's a long way down to the floor in proportion to the baby's size.

Put your baby in the crib when you are called away— even if it's "just for a moment."

Yes, occasionally you may place your child on your own bed—when diapering him, for example. But it's a safe place *only* if you don't take your eyes off him.

4

2. The kitchen floor is *not* a safe place for your toddler. A pot handle carelessly turned outward might be accidentally brushed by your arm, sending scorching food cascading downward. There might still be a sliver of broken glass down there left from the bottle you broke the day before. An appliance cord may be hanging down just far enough from a counter to be grabbed, sending a heavy object over the edge onto a little victim below.

Give your child some blocks or crayons to play with and let him sit in his (sturdy) high chair and watch you cook. You'll both enjoy the time of meal preparation more.

3. The bathtub. Infants and toddlers *can* drown in an inch or two of water. All they have to do is roll over and immerse their nose and mouth. They don't know what's happening to them, do not react instinctively, and are unable to help themselves.

If you are called away while bathing your child, just take him out of the bath and carry him with you. Wet spots on your wood floor are a small price to pay for his safety.

Finally, we come to toddlers and fires.

4. A fire is a welcome sight in the fireplace on a cold winter's night or in the barbecue pit on a balmy summer evening. Don't assume, though, that heat will deter a very young child from putting her hand near the flames. She doesn't automatically jump from cause to effect. What she sees are bright, glowing coals and sparks. To her it's a marvelous sight—something to be further explored. Our *adult* minds tell us to stay away from the flames, but kids aren't adults. They don't reason or act as we do. In fact—they usually *just act.*

At the very least, put a safety screen up in front of your fireplace.

The purpose of these True/False statements was to show you that safety precautions are not always "obvious" to adults. To protect the very young, we must learn to see the world from their perspective. This means experiencing our surroundings from an unfamiliar angle.

Keep your mind and your eyes open, as you read ahead and make your world a wonderful, safe place for your youngsters to enjoy and explore.

THE BEDROOM

The baby's basic angle is zero degrees. He is flat on his back and all the world is up. Or he is turned on his stomach, which makes the world go the other way. When on his stomach, an infant may not have the coordination and strength necessary to extract himself from a position in which his nose and mouth are pressing into his pillow. Nor does he necessarily have the ability, when lying on his back, to lift a pillow or other soft object from his face. Avoiding this state of affairs is simple. Just don't give your baby a pillow to sleep on until he can obviously raise his head. During that early period in his life, you should be careful about *anything* that is put even briefly in the crib.

The Crib

The crib itself must meet certain standards to ensure your baby's safety:

1. The mattress should fit snugly enough against the slats and both ends of the crib so that the baby can't wedge her head into the space. Her bones are still supple, and she can accomplish wonders in this respect.

2. The slats themselves should be a maximum of $2\frac{3}{8}$ inches apart. Broken slats should be replaced immediately.

6

3. Cribs manufactured since 1978 will not present a problem with regard to toxic paint, but if the crib was bought before that year, or if you're not sure when it was made, you must repaint it with nontoxic paint.

4. The crib's mattress should never be covered with thin plastic, which may be easily torn and could possibly suffocate your child.

5. The height of the crib's sides, when fully raised, should always be at least three quarters the height of the crib's occupant. When she grows taller, it's time to get her a bed.

Some cribs have decorative corners called finials, which make for a cutout design on the corner posts. These should be removed, as a baby can sometimes wedge his neck into the cutout. Check all the crib's hardware before you use it, so there is no danger of anything giving way, creating the conditions in which a child's head can become wedged between two parts of the crib.

Toys

Now let's look at the toys that go in the crib. Balloons are *not* appropriate. The bright color and interesting texture will almost certainly cause an infant to put the balloon in his mouth. A balloon bursting that close to his face can hurt. More important, he may chew off a piece which could lodge in his throat. Furthermore, any string is a potential hazard to an infant, both because it can strangle and because it could come loose and be swallowed.

Check for loose buttons or bits of plastic sewed on for eyes, for example, on stuffed animals. Make sure the toy is sturdy enough not to be torn apart by the child. Anything painted should be labeled "nontoxic."

The Good Housekeeping Seal of Approval, while accorded to manufacturers who do, after all, advertise in that magazine, is still a reliable guarantee that the product has been carefully tested for safety.

However, no matter who has tested the product, possible dangers inherent in the toy may become apparent only *after* extensive use. If you think it doesn't look right after considerable wear, don't hesitate. Throw it out.

Playpens

What about playpens? Mesh playpens are fine if the mesh openings are no bigger than ¼ of an inch. Measure the opening to be sure no button can get caught in it. Never use a playpen with one side down. That creates a meshed area between the floor of the pen and the lowered end that is just big enough for an infant to smother in should he fall the right way.

Other Hazards

When baby becomes toddler, it behooves you to see the world from her point of view. Get down on your hands and knees to explore from this perspective. One of the first things you will notice is a wall outlet. Your hardware store sells inexpensive plastic protectors that plug into outlets that are not currently in use, rendering them harmless.

Anything at this level with a sharp edge on it is potentially dangerous, including the edge of the bed frame and other protruding furniture parts. You may also observe low-hanging cords from drapes or Venetian blinds, which should be tied up out of the reach of curious fingers. The same goes for appliance cords that may be hanging down within reach (and check to see that they are not frayed). Also, examine every large object to make sure that it can't be knocked down or pulled over by the movements of a young explorer.

A baby's logic tells him that anything that fits in his mouth ought to be there. There shouldn't be anything small, sharp, or broken on your floor. Nor should there be anything the child can swallow. Be especially attentive to seemingly large objects that can be broken up into bite-size pieces.

If you're using an old toy chest, add safety hinges (standard equipment on newer models), which keep the top from slamming shut. And cut some air holes in the chest, just to be safe rather than sorry.

That toy chest, and any other object that can be climbed on, should be kept away from windows. Your child doesn't know the concept "outside"; windows don't mean the same thing to her that they do to you. In some cities, such as New York, landlords are required to provide free window guards. If you live in a private house or in an apartment where the burden is on you to provide this protection, consider it worthwhile insurance.

A BEDROOM CHECKLIST

The Crib and Playpen

☐ No pillow, plastic covers, or finials.

☐ A mattress that fits snugly.

☐ Slats no more than 2⅜ inches apart; mesh openings no more than ¼ inch.

☐ Fresh paint if older than 1978.

☐ Keep all sides up when child is in crib or playpen.

Toys

☐ No balloons or strings.

☐ Check all buttons and other attachments.

☐ Be sure paint is nontoxic.

The Room Itself

☐ Check it from toddler's vantage point.

☐ Cover outlets and sharp edges and keep room free of low-hanging cords and small or broken objects.

☐ Add safety hinges to toy chest and store it away from the window.

THE BATHROOM

The Tub

When your baby is in the water, anywhere, always hold him and never take your eyes from him. The regular tub is really too big for him; a plastic tub or basin is safer and easier to handle. Keep the water at 125 degrees Farenheit or less. Test the water with your elbow—it makes an excellent thermometer. And remember, if you are called away while bathing your baby, carry him with you.

The Medicine Cabinet

The 1970 Poison Prevention Act was responsible for the child-proof bottle caps on medicine that give adults so much trouble when they try to get them open. They obviously work and have accomplished their purpose. But that purpose can be defeated if you transfer pills or liquids to another container and leave them where a young child can get at them.

While most toddlers probably can't as yet climb up to the medicine chest, it won't be long before they're within grabbing distance. Now is as good a time as any to put a lock on that cabinet door—and keep all razor blades firmly locked in it. Throw old ones out immediately.

A BATHROOM CHECKLIST

☐ Don't leave baby or toddler alone in bathroom.

☐ Lock cabinet doors.

STAIRS

Your stairway can be safe—if you safeguard it!

First, be sure you don't leave your baby in a stroller near the top of the stairs. The same holds true for your toddler in his baby walker. These devices "are not baby sitters," as the Chairperson of the Consumer Product Safety Commission recently pointed out. Baby walkers with wide bases are likely to be the most stable, but no matter how they are built, children should not be put in them if unattended—and not near stairs even if you are there.

Take special care when you carry your baby upstairs or down. You're carrying something precious! Be sure the stairs are well lit—with switches at both the top and bottom of the flight—and that any carpeting on them is secure, and that you have a sturdy railing at the right height.

Gates

The most likely way a baby will get on the stairs is to crawl onto them. Gates at the top and bottom of the flight of steps will keep a young one away from this danger. Don't get the gates with a diamond-accordion pattern and "V"'s at the top and bottom. Those openings are actually wide enough to strangle a baby. Any gate that comes in contact with a young child should have tiny openings, on the same principle that applies to crib slats and playpen mesh.

A STAIRWAY CHECKLIST

☐ Use mesh gates at top and bottom.

☐ Be sure the stairway has: a light switch at both top and bottom, secure carpeting, and sturdy rails.

☐ Never leave a child unattended in a walker or carriage.

THE KITCHEN

In the kitchen, it's the small mistakes you have to watch.

Few parents would let a child touch a hot stove or a pot of boiling water, but there are other ways an infant or toddler may get burned or scalded—from a carelessly held cup of coffee or tea, for example, or from a lit cigarette left in an ashtray. Be careful—and your child will be safe.

Sharp Objects

Sharp objects belong in a drawer or locked cabinet when not in use. These include corkscrews and scissors as well as knives and forks. And throw away any opened cans! That jagged-edged top is at least as sharp as a knife.

High Chairs

Make sure your high chair is safe, solid, and sturdy. The straps on that chair must hold the child securely but comfortably so that he doesn't slip between tray and seat. Like the base of the walker, the lower part of the high chair should be wide enough to ensure stability. If you have other children, make sure they don't think of that chair as a toy to climb on, especially when baby brother is in it!

Babies do not have the chewing and swallowing capacity of older children. Consequently, their ability to handle hard food is limited. That means avoiding foods such as nuts and hard candy, until you're sure she can handle them. (Choking is the leading cause of death at home for children under the age of five.)

Other Hazards

Common sense applies to everything else in your kitchen. Protruding pot handles should be pushed back. Anything spilled or broken should be thoroughly cleaned up. Appliances in use should not have their cords dangling over a counter edge. When not being used, those appliances should be disconnected.

Child-proof all cabinets and cupboards with latches that you can find at any hardware store. Be sure you lock up all your poisonous substances, including ammonia, bleach and detergents, insect sprays and rodent poison, oven and drain cleaners, and any type of polish. (This, of course, holds true for equally poisonous substances, such as mothballs, turpentine, and the like, that may be found in other parts of the house.)

A KITCHEN CHECKLIST

- ☐ Keep sharp and heavy objects in child-proof drawers or cupboards.
- ☐ Put pots and appliances on the back of stove and counter.
- ☐ Lock up all poisonous substances.
- ☐ Be sure high chair is sturdy and solid.
- ☐ No nuts or hard candy for children under five.

THE LIVING ROOM

You will soon expect your young child to put his or her own toys away—so, why not start by being a shining example yourself! You will also save your child from some nasty accidents. Adult "toys" to put away before your child enters the living room include: liquor in open bottles, intriguing but lethal guns, and bright, shiny needles. You might also reconsider buying that glass-topped coffee table with the sharp corners until your baby is beyond the tripping and stumbling stage.

Plants

Most people like plants; so do most babies. The vegetation smells interesting, and the color and texture may invite further inquiry. You would be satisfied to touch and sniff the plant, but your young one has another way of appreciating attractive flora, and that's to put it in his mouth and taste it.

The following plants are common—and poisonous:

Amaryllis	**Ivy**
Anemone	**Jerusalem Cherry**
Autumn Crocus	**Jessamine**
Azalea	**Jimsonweed**
Baneberry	**Lantana**
Bittersweet	**Larkspur**
Black Locust	**Lily-of-the-Valley**
Bleeding Heart	**Lobelia**
Bloodroot	**Mistletoe**
Buttercup	**Monkshood**
Caladium	**Moonseed**
Castor Bean	**Mountain Laurel**
Christmas Rose	**Narcissus**
Crown-of-Thorns	**Nightshade**
Daffodil	**Oleander**
Daphne	**Philodendron**
Dieffenbachia	**Poinsettia**
Elderberry	**Pokeweed**
English Ivy	**Privet**
Foxglove	**Rhododendron**
Glory Lily	**Rhubarb**
Golden Chain	**Virginia Creeper**
Holly	**Water Hemlock**
Hyacinth	**Wild Cherries**
Hydrangea	**Wisteria**
Iris	**Yew**

A LIVING ROOM CHECKLIST

☐ Clear liquor bottles, guns, sewing paraphernalia, and other potential dangers away.

☐ Remove all poisonous plants.

THE GREAT OUTDOORS

It's a good idea to introduce a child to nature at the earliest possible age. She shouldn't be afraid of the outside world and its delights, although she will gradually have to develop a healthy respect for those aspects of the natural world that are inimical to her good health.

Animals

Animals should not be objects of fear for a child. If you don't have a pet, show the child how to be affectionate when you encounter someone else's dog or cat. If you do own an animal, make sure your boisterous toddler learns to love it properly and doesn't treat it like a rag doll.

Even a good dog may not be overjoyed with a new baby in the house, which he may view as a rival "sibling." To make sure that the dog doesn't take out his unhappiness on the child, pamper your pet, just as you would an infant's older sibling. Show the animal that, while the family has grown, his place in your affections is secure.

If you let your child crawl around outside in an area to which your animal also has access, remember that baby, whose sensibilities have not yet been refined, is likely to grab and put in his mouth anything. *Any*thing!

Conveyances for the Baby

Like cars, strollers should be "test driven" before they're purchased, preferably with the child who will use it. Check for stability, sharp edges, and any part of the mechanism in which delicate little fingers may get caught.

Papooselike frame backpacks are also a convenient way to carry a child when you need to have your hands free. Babies over the age of four months usually tolerate them well. Don't use them with younger infants, whose necks have not yet developed the strength to cope with the bumps caused by an adult's normal walking pace. Check to make sure that the straps properly restrain the child without binding her. Any part of the frame that may come near her face should be padded. If you bend over, remember to do it from the knees to avoid the possibility of dislodging, or at least seriously upsetting, your precious cargo.

All children should, of course, be buckled in when traveling in a car, but baby's seat differs from those of her older siblings. It's bucket shaped and faces the rear for the ultimate in protection. She shouldn't be facing forward until she weighs about forty pounds, and even then she should remain in the bucket until she is capable of sitting up straight under her own power.

A CHECKLIST FOR OUTDOORS

☐ Pamper your pet.

☐ Don't leave your baby alone with him.

☐ Check strollers and backpacks for comfort and safety.

☐ Keep children in car seats.

2
TEACHING SAFETY

Tell me, I forget.
Show me, I remember.
Involve me, I understand.
—Ancient Chinese Proverb

Protecting an infant or toddler from harm is a one-sided operation: It's all up to you. But when your child begins to talk and walk, *instruction* becomes part of the shield that will keep the child safe. At this point, you're offering him not only protection but also the tools with which he will ultimately protect himself.

THE PSYCHOLOGY OF TEACHING SAFETY

The Parent-Child Relationship

There must be a special relationship between parent and child if the child is to grow into an adult who can take care of himself on his own. That partnership needs to be based on something solid, enduring, and mutually satisfying.

19

Sheer power just won't do. In fact, the ingredients that will make this partnership work are the ties that bind in any good parent-child relationship: love and trust.

A child who loves and trusts his parents will listen to them most of the time and, for the most part, take what they say to heart. Even when he disagrees vehemently about some limitation they have put on his activities for safety's sake, he will assume deep down that they have his own good in mind.

How do we, as parents, ensure that our own feelings of love and trust will be reciprocated by the child?

- By taking him and ourselves seriously.
- By respecting his feelings and intelligence.
- By constantly reminding ourselves that we are human and bringing our own history and state of mind to the relationship.

We begin by realizing that each child is unique. There's no such thing as the generic "child." Your seven-year-old may have been a rambunctious preschooler, forever seeking out trouble. But her two-year-old brother could be more on the fearful side, almost phobic in his avoidance of things he perceives as "dangerous" to his well-being. He may also be less physically coordinated, a slower learner, and not quite as bright as she was at his age. His playmates, your rivals for influence over him, are not the same as hers. And he has an older sibling, a problem or benefit she may not have had. You may also be living in a different place than that which formed the environment for her earliest years. In other words, the world may look substantially different to him, and the way you talk about it will have to be geared to his own situation, personality, and abilities.

What to Teach?

What are you trying to teach the child? True, he does need information about specific dangers and ways to prevent them or deal with their consequences if they can't be headed off. But you can't anticipate every possible accident that may befall him in what we trust will be a long life. What a child needs to learn more than anything else is *good judgment.* Your goal is to raise an individual who can ultimately deal with any situation and take care of herself. Sociologist David Riesman once described the average nineteenth-century inhabitant of Western countries as having a kind of inner gyroscope. He meant that such a person was less sensitive to what others thought of him than we are today. Our predecessors were, it seems, less dependent on external signals and circumstances and more guided by general principles and their own judgment. They behaved according to values they carried within themselves.

A child who is sensitive to her own safety has an effective "gyroscope" that helps her get her bearings, stay on course, and navigate past the rocks—by herself.

How to Teach

You give your child this ability by teaching her effectively. As she grows, your methods must change. Your authority in her early years comes from your greater age, size, and legal and moral responsibility. But then, as the child begins to develop a mind of her own, it comes from the child's acknowledgment, if ever so begrudging, that you are making sense and describing reality accurately.

A toddler's first misdeeds may reasonably be met with a straight "no." And she may have to be restrained physically from doing something dangerous if she won't take no for an answer. But that's not sufficient for a child with whom you can have a conversation. To get her coopera- tion, you have to tell her *why not.* And the reason should not be because she will be punished by you if she contin- ues to do it. Self-sufficiency will never come if your child becomes obsessed with merely placating you.

Here are ten effective rules for you to follow in teach- ing your children safety and making safety precautions a part of their lives.

1. Make your rules clear and administer them con- sistently. To be respected, safety rules must be spelled out. If your son did something dangerous that resulted from a circumstance he had never before encountered—and about which you had not warned him—he didn't break any rules. Point out the safety principle involved and help him incor- porate it into his growing sense of competence.

Your daughter should know that if something is wrong, it's wrong every time. If you've told her not to cross the street in the middle of the block, don't let her do it even if she's late for school, there are no cars coming, or you're watching from the other side of the street. When she's older, she may be able to employ the rule flexibly. But if she's six years old and just finding her way in the world, your rules should be absolute. And *you* should follow them, too—at least, in her presence.

2. Reinforce your instructions positively. Emphasize the way the child has maintained good safety habits. Don't harp on her occasional failures. When she does break a rule, point out how similar behavior has hurt her in the past—but be quick to add that she has usually taken care of herself very well. Remind her that she has gained greater privileges and responsibility by obeying the rules.

22

3. Respect your child's sense of justice. Kids have an acute sense of when something is *unjust*. They need good explanations for your rules and the way you apply them. If John can't ride his bike to the park while older sister Miriam now has that privilege, he wants to know *why*. Never mind that you've been through this before. Explain once again that she has more experience and knowledge and has demonstrated over time that she can responsibly handle the privilege.

Does he want to know why Roberto, his friend across the street (who's actually a few months younger than John), is allowed to build a tree house and he can't? Explain to him that each family has a different set of rules and that you made yours out of your love for him. No, it's not the perfect explanation, but it's the truth, and there's nothing in it to make John feel bad about himself or you. Although he still may not like it, he will at least finally accept it.

4. Acknowledge the power of peer pressure. Your child may look to other children as authority figures, especially if they're older. Even among preschoolers, the group can be like a god. If your child's playmates say something is all right, she may have a hard time resisting, even if she knows it's wrong or dangerous. She may also find herself put on the spot by a dare.

Don't belittle your daughter's need for acceptance. If her safety is at stake, explain gently why she can't give in to her friends' demands. Show her that other people are trying to force her to do something that is not good for her. Focus on the other kids' insecurities and your own child's strength. She needs to know that she is not being odd or weak. If the problem persists, try talking to the parents of the other kids. They'll probably be grateful to know that their children are flirting with danger and need a talking-to.

Above all, don't panic. To help your child feel strong in this dilemma, you have to show her that you believe in her own innate strength and in the strength of your bond with her.

You can't completely control a child's environment— but you can get a good sense of what outside influences are affecting his judgment. Try to get to know the parents of your children's friends. Are they more permissive than you? Do you notice safety hazards around their house? Do they stress safety awareness in their children?

You can also help *create* your son's or daughter's peer group, especially when your children are young. One New York City mother recently mused that hauling her child off to the playground had some of the quality of going to a singles bar: That way of choosing the child's companions was a bit too random for her. Before her child was born, she had met regularly in a support group with other mothers-to-be. The group continued to meet after their babies were born—with the children—and in a few years they realized that, without planning it, they had formed a playgroup of preschoolers. This gave them some control over which kids might be influencing their children, and it also provided a much needed social outlet for themselves.

5. Listen and respond to your child's objections. As long as what he says has any logic to it, you need to deal with it. If you think it's reached a point where your child is indulging in compulsive game playing, point that out to him. But if he finds a genuine hole in your argument, own up to it. Not doing so destroys your credibility and under-mines your authority.

6. Don't let your child play games with you. Most children try to find out how far they can go. If you think you've spotted that ploy, tell your child. Testing is often a child's attempt to see if you really love her and will keep her from hurting herself.

7. Recognize that you are quite possibly making your child very angry—and accept it. Your are, after all, frustrating him, even if it's for his own good. That's something you can't afford to worry about. If you're feeling guilty and are anticipating his hostility, you may send out a double message in your tone of voice and use of body language. He'll probably pick up your ambivalence and interpret it as a signal that you don't really mean what you said.

8. When necessary, use sanctions to enforce a safety rule. The best kind of sanctions are usually those that suspend a privilege. This can range from not being able to ride a bike for an afternoon to having to go to one's room and forego play altogether for a while. The punishment should, of course, fit the "crime." It may also make the biggest impression if you can somehow relate it to the infraction. For instance, you could suspend bike-riding privileges if the bike was misused.

9. Treat accidents as—accidents! Since no one is at fault in a genuine accident, sympathy rather than punishment is the appropriate response. Tell your child that you're glad she wasn't hurt more seriously. Then, while the hurt is fresh, this might be a good time to review what you've been teaching her about safety precautions that relate to the problem she's just had.

Some kids are accident-prone. Their frequent "accidents" may actually be a call for attention from you. Don't panic. Give your child the regular positive attention he is crying out for—and watch the accidents disappear.

10. Don't underestimate your child. Just as there is no generic child, there is also no unalterable way your child "is." A kid who seems reckless at the age of three may become a very responsible child at five. To draw her along the road to adult freedom, challenge her, when it seems appropriate, to take on greater responsibility.

MAKING SAFETY FUN

For preschoolers, story-telling is often the most effective way of teaching. Here are some ways to make your safety stories work:

- *Make up the stories yourself.* Each one can have a moral about regard for safety and the consequences of ignoring it. It's a good idea to make your child the protagonist of the story and include some real incident that happened to him or her.

- *Get your child to participate by adding to the story or making up one of her own.* She might want to use a favorite doll to make a point. You could even have her and her friends make up a short skit relating to safe behavior.

  A side benefit of this is that, if you're attentive, you may pick up a good deal of information about a child's attitudes as she acts them out—attitudes that might not surface in any other way. In fact, this is one of the approaches psychotherapists use when dealing with children.

- *Act out a story about safety.* It can be either one you have made up or one based on real circumstances. For example, if your child has left things that can be tripped over lying around on the floor of his room, show him what could happen by pretending that you have walked into his room unaware of the objects on the floor and then fake a fall. Ham it up to make your point.

Books

There are many children's books that deal with this subject, and the children's librarian at your local branch library is a good source of information about them. The library may also have a story-reading hour and other activities that are relevant to teaching safety. If it doesn't, suggest that they come up with some.

Television

Television is a mixed bag when it comes to teaching safety. The cartoons, particularly, are negative. They portray characters doing dangerous things which they magically survive. Even when they come crashing down from a tall tree, their wounds usually don't appear to be too debilitating, and often they escape with at worst a dazed expression. It is, after all, supposed to be funny.

Be aware that impressionable children may take these episodes to be representations of reality—and may try to act them out.

Fortunately, there is better fare available. *Sesame Street* is the most notable educational television program that sometimes deals with safety, but the public broadcasting station in your area and local commercial channels may have others.

Games

Games are also useful for older children. Safety games are available where toys are sold, but you can also make up your own. Here are some good ones:

1. Make up a variation of those placemats for kids you often see in roadside fast-food restaurants—the ones with a picture containing a number of mistakes that the child has to discover. Draw a picture in which there are some safety hazards—toys left near the stairs, a child crossing against a red light, a little kid playing with matches. Keep score and give a prize for finding a maximum number of mistakes. Encourage the child to create a similar drawing and have her challenge you.

2. Make up safety lists. This is something that you might do on a long car trip. Ask your son to name as many safety precautions as he can involving playing on the playground. Then ask him to list all the possible hazards that can be found in the kitchen.

3. Play "What if . . . ?" games. These involve inventing scenarios and then posing them to the child to see what she might do. You can use them to test or reinforce your child's knowledge of safety. For instance, you could ask:

- "What if you were just getting out of the bathtub, you were alone in the house, and the phone rang?" (Good answer: "Calmly dry yourself off, put on slippers and a bathrobe, and *then* answer it. If it stops ringing—never mind, the person can call back!")

- "What if you were running for the school bus and the bus door started to close?" (Good answer: "Turn around and go home.")

- "What if a small grease fire started and your younger brother ran to the sink to get water to pour on the flames?" (Good answer: "Stop him! Then turn off the stove, put baking soda on the fire, if you can, and call the fire department.")

CHILD PARTICIPATION

Ideally, your child should gain mastery over her environment by taking on as much responsibility as she can at any given age. One way to help her do this is to have her participate in the setting of family safety policy, the rules by which she will have to live.

For instance, you can name a particular room in the house and then let her have first crack at pointing out the danger spots and suggesting safe procedures to be followed in that room.

Another way that kids can participate in making your home a safer place is by helping you take a safety inventory. Have them check fire hazards in the home. Give them a checklist and send them through the house, attic to basement, looking for dangerous objects or conditions. You could make a contest of it, with a prize for the winner.

Families with more than one child have a built-in opportunity for teaching safety. Ask an older child to watch you care for an infant or toddler. Point out the precautions you are taking and tell your child why you are taking them. Remind him of how much more advanced he is than the baby and how much more responsibility he has for his own safety. Use occasions such as bathing the baby to reinforce bath safety rules for the older child. If possible, let the older sibling help out in caring for the baby—with you close by his side!

In a family with two or more siblings past the toddler stage, the older kids should be encouraged to be role models for their younger brothers and sisters. They'll love being heroes and will find safety principles much more acceptable when they appear as the burdens of knighthood!

A SAFETY INSTRUCTION REVIEW

How to Teach Your Child Safety

- Make your rules clear and administer them consistently.
- Reinforce your instructions positively.
- Respect your child's sense of justice.
- Acknowledge the power of peer pressure.
- Listen to your child's objections.
- Don't let your child play games with you.
- Recognize that you may be making your child angry— and accept it.
- When necessary, use sanctions to enforce a safety rule.
- Treat accidents as accidents.
- Don't underestimate your child.

Making Safety Fun

- Tell preschoolers safety stories:
  —Make up stories, using your child as the protagonist.
  —Have your child add to the story or make up and act out a story of her own.
  —Act out a story yourself.

- Make up safety games for older children:
  —Make place mats with pictures containing safety mistakes.
  —Have children make safety lists.
  —Play "What if...?" games.

Encouraging Participation

- Have children help set safety rules for the house.

- Let them take a safety inventory.

- Let an older child watch and help you with a younger one.

- Make the older ones role models for their younger siblings.

3
MAKE YOUR HOME SAFE ALL YEAR LONG

Your home is your family's haven. It's the place where everyone feels safe. The best way to keep it safe is to take a regular safety inventory. This means simply checking each part of your house for dangerous objects or practices and, if you find any, deciding what to do about them.

A safety inventory is a family activity that will help you root out home hazards while having a lot of fun. How much fun you have is up to you! You can offer prizes to the person who finds the most valid opportunities to improve safety. You can turn the inventory into a treasure hunt, where you give hints on what to look for and let your kids figure out the rest. Use your imagination, and you'll enjoy it as much as the children do.

Give the whole thing the flavor of an Easter egg hunt. You might lead up to it over a period of time, with the big day (or days) held out as the culmination of a number of lessons in safety. Those lessons could be organized around rooms—the kitchen, the bathroom, etc.—or types of objects—sharp objects, electrical objects, and so on. However you organize these lessons, they will prepare your child to understand as well as enjoy the inventory.

How do you do a safety inventory? Here are some suggestions:

1. Make a large chart for each room or category of objects. For preschoolers, draw simple pictures next to the words. Next to each entry, put colored circles containing a "code" symbol that shows whether or not that item is safe. Your code could consist of pluses and minuses, numbers (1 = safe, 2 = unsafe), or a little face with a smile indicating everything is as it should be and a frown designating an unsafe condition or habit. If the child can read, you might just write "YES" or "NO" in the circle.

A list for the kitchen might begin like this:

- Refrigerator

- Stove

- Oven

- Floor

- Toaster

When these items are checked in the inventory, the list might show:

- Refrigerator +

- Stove – (grease build-up behind range)

- Oven +

- Floor – (slippery spot near refrigerator)

- Toaster – (frayed wire)

34

2. Gear the extent of any activity to the age of the child doing it. A four-year-old can't assimilate as much as a seven-year-old. If more than one child is participating, structure the hunt to offer activities appropriate to different ages. Since it may get competitive, be sure the older child doesn't have an advantage. If you're giving prizes, make certain everyone gets something.

3. Use your good judgment when instructing your child. Pointing out unsafe practices to a young child could possibly give that child some "ideas" about trying them. Although this is unlikely, you are the one who knows your child's personality best, so use your discretion.

4. Encourage your child to add to your safety list. You may be pleasantly surprised at his powers of observation.

5. Invite the neighbor's kids in and make a big deal of it. Better yet, plan it as a neighborhood event in cooperation with families in other houses and possibly the library, school, church, or synagogue. You can award a prize for the safest house in the neighborhood.

Now we'll look at the inventory, room by room.

ANYWHERE IN THE HOUSE

- *Check floors for hazards.* Nothing should be left lying around where someone could trip over it. This rule applies especially to areas where children are likely to play.

- *Make a note of exposed points and sharp edges on furniture.* All children occasionally get carried away with their games and will run through the house paying little heed to anything in their way. Some of these hazards will not be obvious to you because you are taller than the child who is at risk. So, get down on your hands and knees to get the lay of their land. If you're making this inventory with a child, have her walk through the house slowly and observe where she might be in danger from protruding objects.

- *Practice learning how to fall.* While you're doing this, you might want to take the time to show your child how to fall, since everyone takes a header once in a while. Show him how to use his hands and arms to break the fall and avoid injury to his face. Teach him to roll over as he hits, to distribute the impact. Have him practice falling outside on the grass. This would also be a good time to stress a safety precaution that will prevent many falls: keeping his shoelaces tied. Or, better yet—buy shoes with Velcro closures.

- *Check your ironing habits.* Do you ever leave a hot iron unattended while you run to the phone or door? Don't. Even if your child can't reach the iron, he can pull on the cord and end up with a bad burn if the appliance falls on him—not to mention an injury from being hit with a heavy object.

  Where do you store your ironing board? Does it block a doorway? If it's in a closet, can it fall out and hit somebody—especially a little person—who opens the closet door?

  The best place to keep your iron and board is a closet with a child guard or safety catch on its door.

- *Examine your space heaters and fans.* The grating over these appliances should be spaced narrowly enough to prevent small hands reaching in. Make sure that your space heater will turn off automatically if it's tipped over.

- *See if there's anything in the house in which a child could lock himself.* Do you have an old chest or trunk stored in the basement? Make certain that it can't be accidentally locked. And, of course, the doors of discarded refrigerators must be removed.

- *Be sure your carpets are nonskid.* Carpets and area rugs must be backed by a nonslip surface. If you have any doubts about a particular floor covering, stand over your child and hold her while she *tries* to make it skid.

- *Cover your radiators and check if they're leaking.* Exposed radiators can cause burns. If they leak, the moisture can make the surrounding area slick, causing a fall.

  Radiators pose another threat, if your child is big enough to use them as a leg-up to the window sill. You can avoid that danger simply by putting something decorative and immovably heavy on top of the radiator.

- *Be sure all locks open from the inside.* Many homes have locks or gates on the windows to prevent burglary. But you don't want these security devices to turn your home into a jail for its legitimate inmates! Be sure they can be quickly opened from the inside. In case of fire, no one has the time to figure out an elaborate lock. Every child in the family should try each window to be sure he can open it.

- *Empty all ashtrays.* Toddlers may reach for the glowing embers or might stick a finger in cold ash and lick it to see what it tastes like.

THE BASEMENT AND GARAGE

- *Check your basement carefully.* If you've moved into a new house, make sure there are no rats in the cellar.

- *Put a lock on your basement door and on closets containing dangerous objects.* Small kids who can reach exposed hot water pipes or oil burners should be kept out of the basement.

  If fuse boxes are accessible to young children, you should either build a lockable box around the fuse box or be sure the children are always under supervision when they're in the basement.

  Have you set up a workshop in the basement or garage? There's no reason why you can't show your youngster the fun of "shop work," provided you stay with him every step of the way! Just be sure you keep control of all those power tools, cutting instruments, nails, and hazardous liquids—and lock them up when you leave.

- *If you use your basement for storage, keep your things in well-secured boxes.* Old appliances, tools, and other knickknacks could hurt small hands not experienced in dealing with them.

- *Tape a safety list over the area in which your child works or plays.* School-age children may have hobbies such as model building for which you have allocated space in the basement or garage. They may also use that area for playing with chemistry sets or engaging in similar activities that require a special space. Make sure your child understands the real dangers of misusing this equipment. And make it an absolute rule that he put away *all* his equipment after he's finished working.

LIVING ROOMS AND RECREATION ROOMS

- *Keep your liquor cabinet locked.* Kids love to imitate what they consider adult behavior. Given the opportunity, they'll almost certainly take a gulp of your gin or vodka.

- *If you own guns, lock them away.* The same goes for ammunition, which should be stored in another place. Don't display the weapons, even in a glass case. They just give your child something to think about.

- *If you have a fireplace, be sure it has a protective grill.* This will keep embers from getting out and little children's fingers from getting in. Older children may be taught how to feed the fire, but make sure you are there when they do it!

BEDROOMS

- *Put anything that can stab, smother, or be swallowed out of reach.* That includes all jewelry, perfume, and cosmetics. The pretty colors and attractive smells may invite careless investigation by little fingers and tongues.

- *Keep mothballs in unopenable containers.* They look remarkably like sucking candy.

- *Get rid of plastic bags.* Contrary to what your child may believe, they are *not* toys. The publicized dangers of suffocation by plastic bags are real.

- *Insist on the proper use of furniture.* A bunk bed is to be treated as a bed, not a trampoline or a castle to be scaled. Use one of your child's toys to illustrate what can happen to someone who starts horsing around on the upper bed!

Electric blankets must be used with care to prevent shock. A child should not use one right after she comes out of the bath. She should not use it at all if she has a problem with bed-wetting.

- *See that all toys are put away and that broken toys are discarded.* Serious accidents have occurred because a child tripped over a toy and hit her head on a dresser or the edge of a bed frame. A jagged edge on a broken toy can also do harm. Since these accidents are so easy to avoid, make clearing-up an inviolable rule.

    A few more notes on toys...

    The child most at risk from an accident involving a toy is a boy between the ages of two and four. When you choose toys, especially for kids of that age, make safety a paramount consideration.

    Don't buy young children toys that make noises loud enough to damage their hearing if held close to the ears.

    And remember, kids should be at least eight before they are allowed to play with toys with projectiles.

THE BATHROOM

- *Keep all medicine out of reach or in child-proof containers.* And always give medicine to a child in a well-lit area, to be sure the substance and dosage are correct. Don't try to coax young children to swallow medicine by saying it's "just like candy." Many cases of aspirin poisoning have occurred because kids heard this invitation and took their parents at their word.

- *Unplug all electrical appliances.* That includes razors, curling irons, and blow dryers. Keep them out of reach of young children, who may try a little misguided experimentation.

Make it a rule that *no one* touches these appliances with wet hands. (Yes—even when they're not plugged in.)

- *Check for stray sharp objects.* Scissors, razor blades, and safety pins should never be left around, even when the kids are older. Since the bathroom is usually used first thing in the morning and just before bedtime, the person using it is likely to be sleepy and not fully alert. If that person is a child who is late for school, she may make a thoughtless movement with her hand that will result in a bad cut from one of those sharp objects.

- *Be sure the tub has a non-slip surface.* You can use either a rubber mat or the patterned bathtub appliqués that may be purchased in any hardware store. Be sure also that there is something to hold on to—at child height—when your son or daughter enters or leaves the tub. And place a nonskid mat on the floor beside the tub.

- *Store cleaning fluids and other caustic substances out of reach or in a locked cabinet.* Do you use "Mr. Yuk" labels on poisonous substances? They've been very effective in repelling small children.

- *Make sure your child can't lock himself in the bathroom.* There should be a way to open the door from the outside. Otherwise, use an inside latch mounted too high for your child to reach.

THE KITCHEN

We covered kitchen dangers in chapter 1. When you make your inventory there, check that:

- Sharp objects are in child-proof drawers.

- Pot handles don't protrude.

- All cleaning substances are locked up.

- There is not grease buildup anywhere.

- All spills are wiped up.

- Faults in floor covering are repaired.

- Frayed wires have been fixed.

- You have explained the dangers of kitchen implements to your child—including the garbage-disposal unit, the food processor, the blender, and the like.

Microwave Ovens

Microwave ovens have not been in use long enough for us to be absolutely sure about the hazards from stray radiation, but as a precaution you may want to keep everybody away from the microwave while it's on. Also, unlike stoves, microwaves have no flame for the child to associate with heat or burning, nor does one feel the heat near the appliance. Food and cooking containers do get hot, however, so potholders are a must.

OUTSIDE

- *Fence in any holes near which your child may be tempted to play.* These include wells, excavations, cesspools—and swimming pools! If possible, fence in the entire backyard to give your child a free but secure playing area.

- *Be sure no ladders are left standing against the house.* Aside from tempting burglars, they may also challenge your child's imagination and sense of adventure and could produce a nasty fall.

- *Lock away all gardening tools.* A child could trip over one and hurt himself badly. Rakes have inflicted nasty facial injuries by slamming up against the people who inadvertently stepped on them. Shears and other pointed or sharp object can cause bad cuts. And chemicals used to treat the soil are as poisonous as those household cleaners you carefully stashed away.

  Small children should *never* operate a power mower. And all children—as well as adults!—should keep a healthy distance from it when it's in motion, to avoid the flying debris.

- *Learn how to start your barbecue with twigs and paper.* A barbecue should be a lot of fun. To keep it that way, don't start the fire with lighting fluid or similar substances that can produce a sudden high flame (and *never* allow kids to use such liquids). Take the time to learn how to get the coals hot with twigs and paper.

  Young children should not be allowed near the fire while food is cooking. The embers must be thoroughly doused when you're finished. When a child seems old enough, let her begin to help you put out the fire. It's a good opportunity to teach fire prevention.

ELECTRICITY

Explain the basics of electricity to your child.

Electric outlets seem somewhat magical to kids, who may be tempted to experiment with them.

A nine-year-old was given an electric game for his birthday. It was a multiple-choice quiz in which he was required to guess the correct answer to a series of questions by placing the tip of one wire on the spot where the question was printed and the other over one of four possible answers. If he chose the spot over the right answer he would complete a circuit and a red light would go on.

His curiosity and increasingly scientific bent led him to wonder what would happen if he put the wires into a wall socket. He tried and instantly got a strong tingling feeling. He also blew out the lights (and destroyed his game). He was lucky; it could have been worse.

That was an unnecessarily hard way to get a lesson. The boy should have been taught about shocks—the right way.

The Electricity Tour

Take your child on an "electricity tour" of the house and explain how to deal with the devices found along the way. Tell him to:

- Be on the lookout for frayed wires.

- Pull out appliances by the plug, *never* by the cord.

- Turn *off* the switch connected to a dead light bulb. He should know that, to avoid the possibility of a shock, you never change a bulb with the switch on.

- Throw away all used batteries from battery-powered toys. He must never toss them into the fire, for fear of explosion. If he wants to know what's inside a battery, tell him it's a liquid called acid, which could hurt him. You could ask his teacher to open one in class as a demonstration.

- Heed all warnings that repairs are to be done only by authorized service people.

Show your child that all major appliances—such as air conditioners and refrigerators—must be grounded. And demonstrate to him that the back of every electrical appliance should be screwed on tight.

Power Lines

Now take him outside. Show him a power line and explain that its enormous voltage can *seriously* injure anyone who goes near it. You don't have to touch the power line directly to get a shock from it. A kite that gets tangled up in it can conduct the electricity down to its holder. Please don't frighten your child away from the wonderful sport of kite-flying, however! Just tell him to keep himself and his kite away from power lines. If the kite does get wound up in the power line, he should let go of it immediately.

Check the power lines around your house to make sure they are securely out of the way—and *always* check them after a severe storm. Downed power lines are extremely dangerous. Caution your child to keep far away from one and immediately report it to you or another adult.

HOLIDAYS

Prepare for the fun and excitement of holidays by doing a quick "holiday inventory" before the big day arrives.

Halloween

Trick-or-treating is a delightful custom that generations of kids have enjoyed. You don't have to scare your kids away from it. But do not allow your child to eat any candy before you have first inspected it. Throw away all candy that is not completely sealed—no matter how small the tear. You will also need to reinforce the notion that pranks are not terribly funny and can cause injury to both the perpetrator and the victim.

An adult should accompany younger children on their rounds, and no child, no matter what his age, should go out ringing doorbells alone. For safety's sake, it is best to confine activity to the blocks surrounding your home, where your children are likely to know the people they are soliciting and where they will themselves be known.

The Fourth of July

You can prepare your children to enjoy the magic of fire-works *without* danger by arranging to take them to a pro-fessional fireworks display. Make the child's viewing of this spectacle conditional on his staying away from any fire-crackers that his friends might have.

Christmas

By checking a few important things, you can make sure your Christmas cheer is unspoiled.

First, the tree. Since you will probably use special lighting that's stored away for eleven months of the year, it's a good idea to give it a trial run. Turn it on for twenty minutes while everybody keeps an eye on it. If it passes that test, you know it's in good shape.

Do you have the base of your Christmas tree in water to slow the drying out process, thus helping to prevent fires? If the tree is tall, set a good example by using a ladder and not a chair to get at the high branches when decorating it. Real candles should, of course, never be lit and placed on the Christmas tree. By all means have the kids help trim the tree, but be sure their efforts don't result in the lights touching the branches or needles. That can happen accidentally if you put other decorations on the tree after the lights are in place, unintentionally moving the lights. Therefore check the tree carefully after all the decorating has been done.

If you have an infant or toddler in the house, bear in mind that small decorations can be swallowed, and that ornaments containing fluid may represent a poison threat. Put those on the higher branches if there are little ones around. Better yet, forego their use until your children are older.

A lit-up tree looks just fine through your window, but the potential for a short circuit and fire is too high a price to pay for that pleasure when you're not around to keep a wary eye on things. When you leave the house or go to sleep, the lights should always be turned off. Involve the kids by appointing them "light marshals," whose duty it shall be to make sure the lights are off and report back to you before the family leaves the house and at bedtime.

FIRE

Here are some fire safety tips from the U.S. Consumer Product Safety Commission:

47

"Remember that children play with matches because they are naturally curious about how things work and because many of them are quite simply enchanted by the flickering of a flame.

"React by satisfying their curiosity. Collect a number of different kinds of matches—book matches, kitchen matches, safety and strike anywhere matches, fireplace matches. Explain to them the usefulness of these matches and why it is dangerous to play with matches: because they might start a fire in the house or burn themselves very badly. These warnings may seem to be too abstract for young children. But most young children have been slightly burned at some point by touching a hot range, plate, iron, etc. Remind them of how much that little burn hurt."

Even when kids get beyond playing with matches, they may still be fascinated by the sight of a roaring fire. You can gratify that fascination by involving them in making a campfire or barbecue.

Undue preoccupation with fire may indicate psychological problems and should be treated accordingly. Children who set fires around the house are more than mischievous; they are acting out strong, disturbed feelings and should promptly get therapeutic help.

Precautions to Take

We've already seen some of the precautions that can be taken against fire in the home—for example, getting rid of frayed appliance cords, and properly screening fireplaces. Here are some others, partly adapted from the U.S. Consumer Product Safety Commission's publication, *A Guide to Flammable Products and Ignition Sources for Adult*

Consumers. You can either incorporate them in your general home safety inventory or check for fire hazards in a separate operation.

FIRE SAFETY INVENTORY

Kitchen

About 65 percent of all home fires start here. We'll look at their four most common causes.

1. Grease. A fire started by burning grease in the stove needs special treatment. DON'T try to fight it with water. It won't work. What you want to do is cut off the oxygen supply to the fire.

If the flames are shooting from the oven and you can get near enough, close the oven door and turn off the gas or electricity. If the fire's on top of the stove, cover it. Salt, baking soda, or sand can extinguish grease fires. It's a good idea to keep a pail of sand near the stove, just in case.

2. Matches. The matches in your kitchen are at least as dangerous as the knives. Keep them safely away from young children.

3. Overloads. It takes only a single spark to start a fire. That spark could come from a short circuit caused by an overloaded circuit or an overburdened extension cord. When in doubt about how much any outlet can take, be conservative. And follow this rule everywhere in the house.

4. Flammable substances. The only thing that belongs near a lit burner is a pot. Do your food preparations away from the cooking area. Impress the importance of this on your children when you begin to show them how to cook.

See that towels are nowhere near the range, and be sure that a breeze can't blow curtains close to the stove, where they could be ignited.

Never reach over a lit stove. To protect your children, check that you haven't stored anything appealing, such as cookies, where they would have to reach over the burners to get them.

Store flammable liquids far from sources of heat. The vapor from aerosols could be ignited, even if the can itself is not in contact with flames.

Finally, every kitchen should contain a small fire extinguisher. Whether or not it should be mounted within your child's reach depends on the child's age and maturity.

Living Rooms, Recreation Rooms, and Bedrooms

Here's a list of fire hazards to watch out for in the most lived-in rooms in your house:

- *Frayed cords.* Extension cords under rugs may become frayed without your knowledge. Check them. Also, take special care not to fray the wire if you're fixing it in place with nails or other sharp objects.

- *Heaters.* Space heaters should be far away from any object that could burn, such as furniture, books, newspapers, or curtains.

- *Home electronic entertainment devices.* Televisions, video tape recorders, and stereo equipment should be well ventilated when in use. Be sure you take all covers off them when you run them.

- *Smoking.* No one should ever smoke in bed—or while lying down on the couch, or anywhere else where he is

MAKE YOUR HOME SAFE

likely to doze off. Tell your child he can feel free to deliver his own safety lecture to either a family member or a guest who violates this rule.

Attic, Basement, and Garage

Clear out these storage areas at least once a year. You don't need a match to ignite a pile of old newspapers. A warm, damp storage area will suffice for spontaneous combustion. Rags and flammable liquids in the garage can be set afire with the smallest spark. If you must store gasoline, keep it only in appropriate containers, and away from your house.

IN CASE OF FIRE

If the worst should happen, and a fire starts in your house, you must be prepared to deal with it. Minutes become precious.

Smoke Detectors

You get those extra minutes by installing smoke detectors throughout your house or apartment. They are cheap and can be bought almost anywhere. Part of your check for fire hazards should be to make sure that the batteries in your smoke detectors are still alive. Your child should accompany you as you test each one. She should also be familiar with the sound they make and be ready to act as if the alert were real, even though the alarms are occasionally set off by something other than fire.

Practice Drills

Obviously, nobody can stay relaxed if there's a fire in the house, but everyone must remain as calm as humanly possible. You can prepare your children for such an emergency by practicing the steps you would all take to ensure that a fire would do minimal damage and not harm anyone.

51

The key to dealing with this kind of emergency is familiarity and routine. Children go through frequent and regular fire drills at school and they should do the same at home. Begin by making a simple drawing of each floor of your house to point out all the possible exits and escape routes. Ideally, there should be at least two ways of escaping from any part of the house. Emphasize the need to get out without stopping to save any possessions. In your drills, walk through all the possible exit routes. Do it often enough so that it becomes second nature to even the youngest children.

Means of Escape

Children (everyone, in fact) should sleep with their bedroom doors closed and windows slightly open. The door will act as a barrier to fire and smoke and the open window keeps the fire from sucking oxygen from the room.

In case of fire, the worst thing you can do is take refuge in a closet. You may well be trapped there.

The easiest way to escape is through the door of the room you're in and on to an exit. But take care. You must first test the door to see what you are likely to encounter on the other side. Feel the door and the doorknob for heat. If they're hot, do *not* open the door. If it feels okay, press your foot and your hip against the door as you open it slowly, prepared to slam it shut if you meet a blast of hot air.

The window on the second or third floor of a private house is another possible escape route. If the firemen are already outside, shout to them to let them know you need help. They'll get you out. A rope or chain ladder will also get you down, but you should have had some practice using it. Ideally, you should try it out in a fire drill.

Don't let your child use the ladder as a toy to play

with in nonemergency situations. She could easily mislay it. If you live in an apartment house, caution your kids *never* to use the fire escape for anything but getting away from a fire. Tell them the elevator is off limits in a fire. The only safe way down is the stairway.

If escape is not immediately possible, here are some precautions to take until an escape route opens or help arrives:

- Cover any vents in the room to prevent smoke from getting in.

- Open the window from the top and the bottom. Smoke will rise and go out through the top and you can breathe from the bottom.

- If you have access to water, wet a piece of cloth and put it in the door crack to slow the spread of the fire and smoke. Also, put a wet cloth over your mouth and nose if smoke does get in the room. Take short breaths through your nose.

- If you have to cross a smoke-filled room, crawl, with your head about 18 inches above the floor.

Extinguishing the Fire

The natural reaction to the discovery of a small fire, even among kids, is to try to put it out. There are times, of course, when that is exactly what you should do. If a match drops from someone's hand and lands on the carpet, your first reaction should be to step on it. The same goes for a small flame that is still manageable. But keep reminding your kids never to pour water on a grease or electrical blaze. Test them on that knowledge with "What if...?" questions.

Tell your children to yell "Fire!" whenever they spot smoke or a flame—even if they're positive they can put it out themselves. A little help never hurt.

If they find they can't put out the fire—and they'll know within seconds—they should call to everyone to leave the building. Tell them not to waste time hauling water from another room or hooking up the garden hose in an effort to play fireman. Instead, they should go straight to a neighbor's house and call the fire department from there.

If you've all had to leave the house, keep a sharp watch on your kids. Head them off if they start to go back into a burning building to rescue a treasured possession.

If a person's clothes catch fire, you must take immediate action. Your kids should know what to do to help themselves or anyone else in this emergency. Here's the procedure.

Gently push the victim to the floor. Then roll him over so as to block the supply of air to the flames. Rolling him in a rug or coat is best, as the material helps smother the flames quickly, but you can also put out the fire by simply pressing the burning clothes against the floor.

If the victim is alone, he should immediately drop to the floor and press the burning side of his body against it. This reaction should be instinctive; that's why you must teach your kids what to do and *repeat* your instructions many times. In an emergency, there's no time to pause and try to remember what to do.

The best remedy of all, of course, is prevention. Stress that your children should never wear loose clothing near a flame. And be sure their clothes, particularly pajamas, are made of flame-resistant material.

ACCIDENTS BY THE CLOCK

Your final safety inventory is a time inventory. Study your kids. When do they seem to have the most accidents? We all have our own bio-rhythms, and most of us have a regular "low spot" during the day. That's the time when we tend to stub our toes, cut our fingers—or take out our miseries on a parent or younger sibling! Note when these times occur for each child.

You'll also find that accidents tend to occur when:

- *A youngster is seeking attention (usually unconsciously).* She may be jealous of a sibling or of some activity that's involving her parent. Accident-prone behavior may be a product of tension between parents, when a child may feel that she's getting lost in the shuffle.

- *The child is getting less supervision than usual.* That may occur if his baby-sitter is negligent or when his mother is pregnant or either parent is ill.

- *He is tired or hungry.* All of which points to late afternoon and early evening, just before dinner, as a time to take extra-special care!

4
IN AN EMERGENCY

Dealing with childhood injuries that may occur in and around the house is largely up to you. But your child can learn to take care of them, too. It's part of the "survival tool kit" she is gradually building up. You can teach her how to get help and administer emergency first aid, so that she can manage well if she is alone or there are no adults around. She can also learn how to help *you*, if you ever need emergency assistance.

POST A LIST

The first lesson in first aid is: learning how to get help. Write up a list of emergency telephone numbers for your child, and establish a permanent place for it next to the phone. Write the numbers clearly, in big, bold numerals. You don't want him to have to fumble for them when time is of the essence. If the list is on the wall, make sure it's low enough for your child to be able to read it.

The numbers you post should include:

- Emergency number for police, fire department, and ambulance (911 in some cities)

- Family physician
- Nearest police precinct
- Poison control center
- Neighbors
- Relatives
- Parents at work
- Child's friends

It's also a good idea to keep a brief medical history of your child next to the phone numbers. This would include anything that might bear on how the child should be treated in an emergency. Among the things that would be listed here are allergies, blood type, and past serious illnesses and injuries.

USING THE TELEPHONE

While teaching a child how to get help, gear the emergency procedure to his age level. A three-year-old may not be capable of calling even one number and getting all the information straight. So you must stick to basics with preschoolers.

The essential information a child needs to be able to give is: his name, his address, and his phone number. Offer him regular practice on this, so the information comes out automatically in an emergency. Otherwise, he may report that his name is "Steven" but become flustered when asked for his last name. A request for his address may produce something like, "next to Betty's house on 15th Street." If you have him repeat his name, address, and phone number two or three times a week, he won't waste precious moments trying to remember them. Stress that his last name is as important as his first. For the address, take advantage of any rhythmic sound it may have to make it into an incantation. The address 37–41, 81st Street, for example, could be drilled into his memory by emphasizing the first syllable of each number. Or you could make up a song or poem using the number. Or it might lend itself to the creation of a mnemonic device. You might even make up a game in which his identifying code is his address. The same methods could be used to teach him his phone number.

Using the phone is a prime survival skill. Children as young as two-and-a-half can be taught it. Even if dialing a number is as yet too complex, your child can be taught to dial "0" for the operator. Highlight that button or hole on the dial using a crayon or bright colored paint to make it easier for the child to recognize. As long as the child stays on the line, even if she can't quite get all the information right, the call can be traced. All she has to be able to say is that her father "fell down and can't get up." In rural areas, because the community is small, the operator may even know the child.

Children can begin to learn to use the phone by playing with a toy phone. Have them practice calling the operator to ask for help. But you should make it clear early on that the telephone is an important object and not a toy. Children should also be encouraged to talk to relatives on the phone, thus gaining an awareness that it is a means to communicate with loved ones, people who care about them.

Young children should feel absolutely free to ask for assistance in an emergency. They need to know that manners go by the boards at such times. Teach them that barging into a neighbor's house in an emergency, for instance, is the right thing to do.

Also, make sure your children realize that there is indeed help all around. If medical help is not immediately available, a pharmacist can give competent advice. In most towns, the police will gladly serve as emergency ambulances. If you don't have the number of the police or fire department, the operator will put you through directly if you dial "0" (or "911," if available in your area) and say, "Police (or fire)—emergency." Your kids should know that these resources are there for them.

FIRST AID

In this section, you will find general methods of treating major emergencies that may occur in and around the house. Except for choking, which can be dealt with on the spot, the goal in all these procedures is to stabilize the child's condition until medical help arrives. As the child gets older, she will learn more first aid to use for the benefit of herself and others. Kids reaching early adolescence are ready for advanced training. At that point, you and your child would do well to take a course in first aid at the Red Cross or another institution.

You can start now by displaying, in a prominent place (on your refrigerator door, for instance), a chart with words and pictures describing the basics of first aid in case of injury. Call your local Red Cross or library to find out how to get one. Even if you feel you know first aid techniques, it's not always easy to keep your head clear in an emergency. If you forget something vital, the chart will prompt you. It's also useful for kids who are just learning how to deal with emergencies.

The Medicine Chest

A well-stocked medicine chest is your damage-control tool. The material in there will bring relief and ease the situation until professional help arrives. Sometimes you won't even have to seek further help.

Here's what your medicine chest should contain:

- Adhesive tape
- Sterile cotton and gauze
- Various sizes of Band-Aids or similar small bandages
- Tweezers
- Scissors
- Thermometer
- First-aid cream
- Hydrogen peroxide
- Antiseptic wipes
- Syrup of ipecac
- Splints
- Large pieces of clean cloth to improvise bandages
- Pain-killing medication
- Safety pins

SHOCK

We deal with this first because it can accompany any major medical emergency. Look for shock as a matter of course when dealing with a serious injury.

Shock is a disruption in the blood system, usually caused by trauma. Symptoms are perspiration, skin that is cool and pale, a weak but rapid pulse beat, and a distant look in the child's eyes. The first thing to do is to reassure the child, which means that you must remain calm yourself. Head injuries excepted, the child should be lying down with his body elevated above his head. Keep him warm, but not hot. Alleviate thirst by moistening his lips. Get a doctor immediately.

BLEEDING

Teach your child not to panic at the sight of blood. If the sight of blood does upset him, part of your job will be to reassure him. If the problem is more than a minor cut, have him lie down and raise the injured part of the body. (This is not applicable if there is any possibility of a fracture.)

Everyone can stand to lose a little blood (as much as half a pint for kids before it gets really serious), and bleeding does perform a useful function in cleaning out a wound.

Treating the Wound

Bleeding can usually be stopped by simply applying pressure on a bandage or clean cloth placed directly over a wound. Usually, within three minutes, the body's clotting function will have stemmed the flow.

If the flow of blood is slow, clean the wound with cold running water and apply a bandage. If the flow is heavy, stopping it takes priority over preventing infection. If you have no bandage, use your hand to press on it. You may have to apply pressure for as much as ten minutes before the bleeding stops. If you apply a bandage and the blood starts to flow again after a while, apply another dressing on top of the old one: Don't remove the original. Take care not to cut off the circulation. After the blood has clotted, use tape to hold the compress in place.

Pressure Points

The next step, if direct pressure doesn't work, is to apply pressure to the body's pressure points, strategic locations through which arteries pass. This is a bit tricky and really requires some practice before you actually do it. Since it is the treatment of preference when direct pressure on the wound alone does not stop bleeding, it's worth taking a course to learn all the details.

If blood is coming from the arm, the point to squeeze is midway between the armpit and the elbow. Your thumb goes on the outside of the arm at that point and your fingers squeeze from the inner side. If a leg is bleeding, the point to squeeze is where the groin meets the upper thigh. Facing the victim, you place one thumb on top of the other and press down, pushing the artery against the pelvis.

Applying a Tourniquet

If the bleeding still continues, resort to a tourniquet. It should be at least two inches wide. Wrap it twice right above the wound, place a stick or similar object on top of it, and tie a knot around the stick, to enable you to turn the stick if you need to tighten the tourniquet. Tighten until the bleeding has stopped. Loosen every fifteen minutes, then tighten again, until professional help arrives. Try to note when you applied the tourniquet—the doctors will probably want to know.

For any substantial wound, even if you've got things well under control, it's a good idea to check with a physician. *Always* consult a doctor about a puncture wound, no matter how small, because of the strong possibility of infection.

Nosebleeds

Nosebleeds are likely to be innocuous, even though they are messy. Usually, sitting, pressing the bleeding nostril against the bone and applying a cold compact to the spot will do the trick. But if it goes on for much longer than fifteen minutes, keep the pressure on and head for a doctor.

FRACTURES

If your child has *any* reason to suspect a fracture, treat it as such. Take special notice when:

- An injury to a bone is very painful

- The bone seems out of shape

- The bone is a different length from its corresponding part on the other side of the body

- The affected area is swollen, bluish, extremely tender, or immovable

Before you treat a fracture, see if the victim is having trouble breathing, is bleeding profusely, or has gone into shock. Treat those conditions first. Then, if no bone is actually showing at the injured spot, apply cold compresses to reduce swelling. Open fractures, in which a bone is clearly protruding through the skin, should be covered with a bandage. No attempt should be made to press the bone back into place.

All fractured limbs should be supported and immobilized as they are—let a doctor do the setting. Use splints, bandages, and slings in a manner appropriate to the part of the body affected. Anything long and rigid may serve as a splint. Make sure it reaches beyond the joints both above and below the break. And be careful not to cut off circulation when you tie the splint in place.

If an injury has occurred to the head, neck, or back and there is any loss of consciousness, difficulty in moving, loss of sensation, or a tingling feeling, assume the possibility of fracture and treat with extreme care. Don't move the child unless his life is threatened by fire or other immediate catastrophe. If you have to move him, do so carefully, immobilizing his head, neck, and back. Paralysis or death could result from mishandling. Get medical help right away.

BURNS

Minor, or first-degree, burns are not terribly threatening to a child's health, although they can be quite painful. They usually result when kids are briefly scalded. In this case, the child's natural reaction would be the right one: Put it under cold water. Clean the area and then apply burn cream or first-aid cream.

Second-degree burns are, literally, more than skin deep. They cause blisters and sores that leak. Cold water is still the first medicine to reach for. After immersing the affected area, take a clean cloth that has been dipped in cold water and squeezed dry and put it on the spot. Continue to refresh and apply the compress until the pain subsides. Bandage the wound and go to the doctor. Under no circumstances should you try to break the blisters.

Third-degree burns are often characterized by skin that turns black or white and exposure of tissue below the skin. Nerve destruction may prevent pain. The danger of infection, shock, and permanent tissue damage from third-degree burns is substantial Clothing that sticks to the burn should be left as is. Very cold water should not be used to treat this level of burn, since it may induce shock. Use cool water and elevate the affected area. If possible, apply a bandage, and get medical attention immediately.

ELECTRIC SHOCK

The child must first be removed from the source of the current. To do this, *do not touch him*—you will not help him and will probably be disabled by the electricity yourself. If you can't turn off the current, you must free him from it by pushing him away from its source. Do that with a dry, nonmetallic object, such as a wooden pole, while standing on a floor or ground that is dry.

Check first to see if the child is breathing. If he isn't, give him mouth-to-mouth breathing assistance. That is: Put him on his back. Make sure there is no object in his nose or mouth preventing breathing. Tilt his head back, support the back of his neck with your hand, pinch his nostrils, completely cover his mouth with yours, and exhale quickly four times. If that doesn't get him breathing again, continue by giving him one breath every three seconds until his chest begins to rise and fall and he is breathing under his own power.

For small children and infants, don't pinch the nostrils. Put your mouth over both the child's mouth and nose and proceed as above.

Circulatory collapse may require cardiopulmonary Resuscitation (CPR), but you need training to do that. (You can get it from either the Red Cross or the American Heart Association.) Also check for burns. Immediate medical assistance is mandatory.

POISON

If your child swallows a poisonous substance, you have to act quickly and knowledgeably. If you're not sure if the swallowed substance was poisonous, you can and should act by assuming it is until proven wrong. But you do need to know what the substance was before giving treatment.

Your immediate reaction should be to give a glass or two of water to dilute the substance. Then phone the nearest poison control center for directions. Have with you the container from which the poison was ingested. Be prepared to answer the following questions (as well as you can, obviously):

- What was swallowed?
- Who manufactured it?
- What was in it (on the label)?
- How much was swallowed and when?
- How old is the child?
- What reactions has the child had?

You may or may not be told to induce vomiting. Corrosive substances can harm sensitive tissue if vomited. Among these are the following:

- Drain, oven, and toilet bowl cleaners
- Floor and furniture wax or polish
- Grease solvent
- Kerosene
- Lye
- Naphtha
- Paint thinner

- Quicklime
- Shoe polish
- Anything containing zinc

Vomiting will not be recommended if the child is unconscious or in acute pain.

If vomiting is required, the best way to induce it is with syrup of ipecac. Give one tablespoonful with a glass of water. If you get no results, try again in twenty minutes. Should another ten minutes pass without vomiting, touch the back of the child's throat with your finger.

Parents should be alert to the fact that not all poisonous substances result in stomach distress. Convulsions combined with psychologically aberrant behavior such as hyperactivity and extreme agitation can be some of the symptoms if your child has swallowed amphetamines, antidepressants, antihistamines, aspirin (a leading cause of childhood poisoning in overdoses), camphor, cold remedies, sleeping pills, strychnine, perfume, after-shave lotion, or tranquilizers. If you suspect any of these, give the child water to dilute the poison, and then call the doctor and tell him your suspicions.

CHOKING

If something lodged in her throat has completely blocked the child's breathing passage, you have a maximum of five minutes to save her life—not enough time to send for a doctor. Reaching into the throat to extract the offending substance may accidentally push it further down. Smacking her on the back may produce the same result. Fortunately, there is an easy, noncomplicated way to quickly clear the obstruction and get her breathing again by harnessing the force of the air still in her lungs to "pop" out the object.

The Heimlich Maneuver

Since 1974, the Heimlich Maneuver, named for its developer, Dr. Henry J. Heimlich, has saved innumerable lives. This technique is safe and simple enough for a child to perform on you or herself. All that's needed is a clear head and arms long enough to stretch around the victim's torso. The choking victim may be ministered to whether she is standing, seated or prone.

If the child is standing, hug her from behind by pressing your fist just below her ribs and above her navel. Your thumb should be against her body. With your other hand, grasp that fist and quickly push it up and into the child's abdomen. This action should be done by bending your arms at the elbow—this is not a bear hug. It may take several of these staccato actions to produce results.

If the victim is sitting, the method is the same as above, except that you will be kneeling behind her. If an infant is choking, hold her on your lap and perform the maneuver.

If she's fallen to the floor, don't waste time trying to get her in a sitting or standing position. Turn her face up and kneel over her with your knees at her hips. Place the heel of your hand where you would put your fist in the other two positions. Place your other hand on top of it and, using your weight, lean forward and press down quickly. If you are in trouble and your child is going to rescue you, this is the best position for her to do it in.

Victims, including children, can help themselves when choking. Arrange with your whole family (and friends and other relatives, for that matter) to give a sign if one is ever choking. The most commonly used is for the victim to place her fingers on her neck. This will save time by providing an instant diagnosis. If you are alone, don't wait until help arrives. Stand and perform the maneuver on yourself.

EYE AND EAR INJURIES

If a corrosive chemical gets into the eye, it could lead to blindness in a matter of minutes. Do not rub the eyes. Flush them with cold water (milk will do as a substitute). If the water is running or is poured on the eye (with the lids held open), it should hit the eye first in the corner closest the nose and run toward the other side. If you have a container already filled with water and his face will fit in it, have the child immerse his eyes and blink his eyelids. Flush for about ten minutes, then keep the eyes closed, put a bandage over them and get him quickly to a doctor.

If something has lodged in the eye, don't attempt to remove it. Cover both eyes with a light bandage, keep the child on his back, if possible, and get him to a doctor.

If a child's ear has been injured by having something poked into it, take him to a doctor. If blood is dripping from the ear, cover it, have him keep the ear facing downward, and get him to a physician. If anything becomes lodged in the ear, seek medical help. You should not try to tamper with anything in the ear canal.

THE CHILD AS RESCUER

We have already seen that even a young child can summon help for a parent or another person who is sick or injured. We've also noted that a child can save an adult from choking to death by performing the Heimlich Maneuver. While you certainly don't want to place too heavy a burden on young shoulders, you really should teach your child how

70

to help in one other serious emergency: a heart attack.

If he is present when a grown-up is having a heart attack, it's quite enough for a younger child to know that something is wrong and that he should call for help immediately. An older child should be able to recognize the obvious signs of a heart attack.

First, he should be able to distinguish a heart attack from a choking incident. A conscious heart attack victim can speak and breathe, at least initially, whereas a person who is choking cannot. Then, he should learn to recognize the symptoms of a heart attack, which are:

- A signal of crushing chest pain that may end up in the shoulder, back, or jaw

- Pale skin

- Nausea

- Perspiration

He should also be prepared, after summoning help, to restore breathing by loosening the victim's clothing and giving mouth-to-mouth artificial respiration.

Most of all, the child should know that in *any* possible medical emergency, if any troublesome symptoms are present, he should call a doctor.

5

WHEN YOU CAN'T BE AROUND

A child needs to realize that there are more than one or two people in the world who can take care of him. He also needs to learn that people responsible for his safety will need his cooperation in seeing that no harm comes to him. Most kids are faced with this early on the first time their parents leave them in the care of a baby-sitter.

School represents another step up the ladder to maturity. Here a child is in the care of adults other than his parents, but as their attention is divided, there is a greater call for him to be sensible and do nothing that could endanger his well-being.

In some cases, usually because of economic necessity, a child may even, in effect, have to temporarily "parent" himself. This is the latchkey phenomenon, in which kids return to an empty house after school because parents are still at work and can't afford alternate-care arrangements. The word comes from the key to the house, often worn around the child's neck, which is the symbol of both his independence and vulnerability. Latchkey kids are often called upon to show maturity beyond their years. Parents can help them bring this off by seeing to it that they have the knowledge they need to keep themselves out of danger.

BABY-SITTERS

Grandparents, aunts, and uncles usually make the best baby-sitters, but they are not always available. Most parents will have to rely on a local baby-sitter, at least occasionally. Here are some guidelines to help you find a reliable sitter and make sure she or he does as you wish.

- Ask friends you respect to recommend a sitter they use.

- If your local school gives baby-sitting courses—as many do—call the school and ask if they can help you find a reliable sitter.

- When you interview the sitter, trust your intuition. If you feel unsure about the person, thank him or her for coming to talk to you—and say good-bye.

- Once you've found someone you like, show her that this is a serious, responsible job. Call home at irregular intervals. Make sure the sitter realizes in advance that this is your practice. If you're hiring an all-day sitter to care for a young child while you're at work, visit her in her home to see if she takes obvious safety precautions.

- Show the baby-sitter your list of emergency phone numbers and make sure he understands what to do in common emergencies. Be sure that *your* name and address are also there. You are not likely to forget that, even in an emergency, but he might. Be sure he knows where you're going to be and at which times. Tell your sitter whom to call first in an emergency (friends or relatives most likely to be home) if he can't reach you.

• Give the sitter a guided tour of the house so that he will know where all the doors and phones are. Make sure he knows where to get a flashlight and any other tool he might need in a pinch. You might even want to introduce him to your next-door neighbors if you know that they will be home during the evening.

Your sitter should fully understand and abide by the "rules of the house." Here are four rules to make clear:

1. Baby-sitting is work. That may seem elementary, but the peculiar conditions of the job might encourage a sitter to make himself feel too much at home: he must stay awake during the entire evening.

2. Under no circumstances may he leave the child.

3. He must not open the door to anyone except you and anyone else you have authorized to be there during the evening. (If you allow him to have a friend over, make sure it's someone you've met, preferably a person with whom he is not romantically involved.)

4. If the child is distressed by anything other than crankiness or separation from you, the sitter is to get in touch with you and call for any other help that may be relevant. Be sure he realizes that in case of fire, his first thought should be to get the child out of the house, then summon help.

When you get home, ask the sitter what he and the child did while you were out, assuming his charge wasn't asleep when he went on the job. A good sitter will be happy to discuss it with you. The next day ask the child about the baby-sitter. Aside from giving you specific information that could be important, you will get a good sense of how comfortable the child feels with the sitter.

When you get a new sitter, tell him *and* your child that he is acting in your place and has considerable authority with regard to your child's conduct. If there are any special instructions for the sitter pertaining to limitations on the child's activities, make sure you present them in the presence of both sitter and child.

SCHOOL

The beginning of school is one of the great divides in life. Other people are now responsible for your child's safety, on a daily basis. However, you still play the primary role in ensuring your child's well-being. For one thing, your child's acceptance of the teacher's authority will depend largely on *your* attitude toward the teacher.

Establish a good relationship with your child's teacher. Make sure your child sees that you have an active interest in her schooling. Discuss it with her. Take advantage of Open School Week and other opportunities to confer with the teacher and other school officials. Volunteer to help out on class trips and other school activities so that the child sees a direct relationship between her care at home and at school. If there are any practices or conditions at school that you regard as inimical to your child's welfare, be active in trying to change them and discuss that, too, with her.

You've put in a lot of time and effort both protecting your child from harm and teaching her the rudiments of how to protect herself. Now she must understand that what constituted safe behavior at home applies to the outside world, as well, when other authority figures are in charge.

Naturally, children can have accidents at school. Statistically, the most likely candidate is a male second-grader engaged in unorganized play in a playground or gym during the middle of the week in the spring or autumn. Can you do anything to lessen your child's risks? Of course!

First, you teach *caution* in situations that clearly represent danger and *good judgment* in grayer areas where discretion is the key. Be sure to relate accident prevention at school to the precautions you take at home. For example, when your child has her first fire drill at school, remind her of how you talked about ways of getting out of the house if there were a fire and how you practiced making quick exits. Explain to her why doing the same thing at school is complicated by the size of the building and the number of children involved. Always point out the differences, but keep the similarities clearly in her mind. She will absorb the new experience best if it's constantly related to the familiar.

If peer pressure didn't influence her behavior before, it will certainly do so now because she is being exposed to a lot more peers. At the first indication that her behavior is being negatively affected by schoolmates, sit down with her and remind her of the questionable motives of kids who want her to do things she shouldn't or doesn't want to do.

Take a special interest in those of your child's classes that may present hazardous conditions—such as shop, chemistry, or even gym. Ask the child to go over the teacher's rules for shop safety. Discuss them as they relate to similar activities at home. By age ten or twelve, for example, children can help out with repairs around the house or garage. See that your child realizes that he must take even greater care at school because there are more children around using more machines with probably less supervision than he gets at home.

By high school, you may have to deal with an adolescent who is obsessed with "going out for the team." If you have any doubts about threats to your child's health posed by a school sport—football is a prime candidate—carefully examine the school's sports program. Do they have sufficient equipment? Is the coach obsessed with winning at all costs to the point where it overshadows good sportsmanship and enjoyment of the game? Do you think your child has a good sense of what his limits are? Is he built solidly enough for a contact sport? If your answer is "no" to any of these questions, find an alternative sport or a sport at another place—say, a club or a "Y"—where both you and your child will be happy.

LATCHKEY KIDS

Approximately half the children in this country do not go directly home after school. Most go off with friends or else participate in organized programs. However, a large number of kids who do go straight home don't find their parents there. Conservative estimates peg the number of youngsters who come home from school to an empty house at over five million. Although no parent wants to leave young children alone, it's sometimes unavoidable.

In many large cities there are social agencies which will suggest alternatives to leaving children alone or ways to help the kids take care of themselves. Many groups have phone numbers that the child can call for practical information and reassurance when her parents can't be reached.

For a list of such organizations, consult *The Handbook for Latchkey Children and Their Parents* (Berkley), by Lynette Long and Thomas Long. It's a useful and inexpensive paperback that covers everything you might want to know about leaving a child alone.

Children should be at least school age before they are left alone, even briefly. The older they are, the more likely they are to stay safe by themselves. Working parents can ease the child's burden by taking advantage of every possible resource. Neighbors, for example, may be willing to occasionally look in on the child, as would a retiree, who might be delighted to have something useful to do.

Safety Precautions

Every safety precaution around the house mentioned so far, of course, takes on greater importance when a child is alone. If you have any doubts about the child's ability or willingness to take those precautions into account, don't leave her alone.

Upon arriving home, the child should check to see that nothing is amiss before she enters the house. If she has any suspicion that someone has tried to break in or that anything else is not as it should be, she should call you from a neighbor's house or a pay phone (she should always carry change for that purpose). Once inside she should never open the door to strangers. She should also tell you in advance about anybody she wants to invite over.

The best way for children to avoid fire is to minimize their time in the kitchen. Young children should not use the stove at all. Leave cold snacks to hold them until you get home. In that way, they won't need to use any of the other kitchen appliances, either.

If you have more than one child staying in the house

79

while you are not there, the older sibling will naturally take on some of the responsibility for the younger. But you need to be careful with this arrangement. Unless that older child is well into his teenage years, he is not really a substitute for you and may not always use his authority with discretion and fairness.

If your child is going to be alone for a time, she should stay in close contact with you. That means using the telephone. The first thing she should do when she gets home is to call you at work. If you're too busy for even a quick "hello," arrange for someone else at work whom she knows to take the call so that at least she hears a familiar voice. If possible, there should be a few more regularly spaced calls until you leave for home.

Safety for the solitary child is important enough that it be spelled out. Formulate the safety rules she must follow and write them on a chart. Go over them with her periodically. Writing can also establish your presence in the house when you're not there. Write her a brief note of greeting every day and leave it for her in a regular place. It will make her feel less alone.

6
VEHICULAR SAFETY

PEDESTRIAN SAFETY

Children should be taught the elements of pedestrian safety
long before they are allowed to cross the street by themselves. For one thing, a young child could get lost and be
forced to cross the street before she is really ready for it.
For another, these rules are so important, so basic, and so
necessary that you must rely on more than just a few heart-
to-heart talks before she's issued her "walking papers."

Begin by explaining to a preschooler why you're waiting at the corner when there are no cars coming. Even if he
doesn't seem terribly interested, come back to it frequently.
(This assumes, of course, that you are willing to set a good
example and obey the laws yourself—an absolute necessity
if you expect to have him obey them when he's on his
own.)

When he begins to get the point, make a little quiz out
of what you've been teaching. When you come to a stop
sign and see a car approaching and slowing down, ask him
why you don't immediately take him across. If he doesn't

correctly answer that you're waiting to see if the car makes a complete stop, remind him of how unpredictable drivers can be, and how a pedestrian always has to play it safe. Use as many mnemonic devices and rhymes as you can come up with (e.g., "Better safe than sorry!").

By the time your child is ready to cross the street alone, he should have a good working knowledge of the range of actual driver behavior, in addition to having assimilated the basic rules of being a safe pedestrian. Those rules are:

1. Take crossing the street as seriously as anything you ever do. It can never be part of a game. It demands your complete attention and seriousness. Horseplay belongs on the playground.

2. Do cross at the green and not in between. But look *both* ways and proceed with care even there. When the light is in your favor, the sign says "WALK," not "RUN."

3. Watch out for bike riders. You can get hurt if you're hit by a bicycle. Bicyclists often ride the wrong way, weave in and out of traffic, and even cut briefly up onto the sidewalk to get around an obstruction. Some are inconsiderate enough to ride their bikes on the sidewalk as a matter of course.

4. Take special care in bad weather and the poor lighting conditions that prevail at dusk. At these times, it's hard for a driver to see pedestrians, especially small ones. They are devoting more of their attention to the mechanics of driving, and therefore may take longer than usual to spot you. Truck and bus drivers may be seated too high off the ground to spot a little kid. Be especially careful when crossing near one of those vehicles.

CHILDREN IN CARS

Seat Belts

The National Safety Council has estimated that more than 3,000 lives are saved annually by seat belts. Many of those are children. Preschoolers and older children need the restraints just as much as their infant siblings. As of this writing, most states have laws stipulating restraints for children up to the age of six, and every state except Wyoming requires children five years old and under to wear seat belts. (New York State now mandates seat belts for everyone in the front seat of a car.)

Fortunately, there has been so much publicity given to the necessity of buckling up that now you are as likely to hear kids reminding their parents about using the belts as you are of hearing parents admonishing their children. If that's not the case in your family, refuse to turn the ignition key until everyone is strapped in. And that includes every trip you take. Statistics indicate that accidents are most likely to occur close to home at speeds under forty miles per hour.

Since the belt must go over the hips, a bolster cushion will be needed until the child is big enough to sit flush on the seat—generally, this applies to children less than fifty-five inches tall. This precaution is important to avoid accidental strangulation and to ensure that the belt conforms to their higher center of gravity. Be sure that, whatever specific restraint configuration you choose for your child, it is adequately padded for safety and comfort. Most kids will need special children's seat belts until they are at least five. They should be strapped into the center of the rear seat unless there are other passengers in the rear. Whatever type of restraint you choose, make sure it's securely anchored to the vehicle. Strap the child in yourself. In four-door cars, be sure to child-proof the rear door locks.

Riding in the Front Seat

When your child is old enough to ride in the front seat (in Germany they are not permitted there until the age of twelve), he must realize what is involved in safe driving. Before he is ever permitted to sit up front, you should begin to make clear the danger of anyone but the driver touching the car's controls—even when the motor is off. Stress, too, how important it is not to touch the controls accidentally. Children can be fidgety, especially on long trips, and are prone to kick their legs and move their arms about indiscriminately, posing the danger of their brushing against a pedal or the driver's arm.

The child should not be encouraged to fantasize that he is the driver. To nip such fantasies in the bud, never purchase child seat/restraint combinations that come with extras such as a toy steering wheel so that the child may emulate the driver. It should also be emphasized that siblings are not to horse around in the car and that children should never distract the driver in any way. If your child is annoying you and you feel you have to deal with his behavior before you reach your destination, don't turn around to confront him: pull over to the side.

Never Leave Children Alone in a Car

Leaving young children alone in a car is asking for trouble. If it's summertime, they could suffer heat stroke or suffocate if you turned off the air conditioning and forgot to open the windows. If you've left your key in the ignition, even a small child might be capable of starting the motor and moving the car, since kids are observant and love to imitate. Even with the motor off and the key removed, they might manage to release the parking brake. So when you get out, take your children with you!

THE SCHOOL BUS

Pity the Poor Driver

If two or three boisterous children can distract you in your car, just imagine how twenty-five excited and frisky kids can affect a school bus driver! All the more reason to emphasize safety-mindedness to kids who ride buses.

Kids in a group are not going to take safety precautions instinctively. On the contrary, they tend to assume that adults will always be willing and able to look out for them and thus magically protect them. Adults have to teach children that the school bus driver is only human and needs their cooperation to ensure a safe ride for all. Much of the responsibility for this belongs with the school. One way schools can fulfill this obligation is to have the driver go in and talk to the kids in their classroom. Each child should also be allowed to sit briefly in the driver's seat so that they can see how the driver's field of vision is not unlimited, especially when it comes to small children.

Elements of School Bus Safety

If school bus safety isn't taught at your child's school, insist that such a program be instituted. Follow it up with your own school bus safety lessons at home. If your daughter has an older brother who's been getting to school by school bus, use some of his experiences to make your points about safe behavior before it's her turn to commute. Relate school bus safety to pedestrian and car passenger safety, with which the child will already have some familiarity.

Here are some standard rules that should be heeded for a safe ride:

• Even if a school bus stop is clearly marked, don't assume that automobile drivers will always proceed cautiously.

• When crossing in front of a bus, make sure you are far enough in front of it so that you can be seen by the driver. Never bend down to pick up something that you have dropped if you are in front of the bus: The driver may not be able to see you. First tell the driver what happened so that she knows you're there.

• Get to the bus stop on time. Rushing means that you are less likely to heed safety rules.

• Line up to board the school bus. Crowding and pushing at the door could cause a child to fall under the bus.

• *Never* cross behind a school bus.

• Don't bother the driver. Follow her instructions. When the bus is in motion, speak to her only if necessary.

• Make sure you know where the emergency exits are.

• Don't clown around on the bus. Hold on if you have to stand. Don't block the aisle with packages, backpacks, or other objects.

• Never stick anything out the window, especially any part of your body.

• Don't throw snowballs at school buses. The driver has enough to watch out for without that diversion.

Recently a movement to put seat belts in school buses has begun to catch on. This has surfaced partly as a reflection of parental concern that safe behavior in private cars with respect to seat belts, achieved after years of legal infighting and heavy public-service advertising, not be undermined by a different set of rules on school buses. If you feel strongly about this, why not raise the issue at the next meeting of your local school board?

BICYCLES

Bicycles are a kid's delight. They are marvelous toys that provide good exercise and *safe,* efficient transportation—if they're used properly.

What to Look for in a Bike

The child should feel as comfortable on a bike as you would want to be in a car. Would you feel safe, not to mention comfortable, in a vehicle in which your feet barely touched the brake pedal or in which your knees were jammed up against the steering column? Would you be satisfied with putting blocks on the pedals so that your feet could reach them? Of course not! So—buy a bike that fits your child *today,* not yesterday or tomorrow.

Hand brakes require big hands and good coordination, so kids under the age of seven should probably be using bicycles with coaster brakes, which they can stop by simply pedaling backwards. Ten-speed bikes would present great difficulties for a young child, who might have to do three things simultaneously: pedal, switch gears, and brake for an emergency stop.

Safety Precautions

The handlebars should be tight and properly aligned with the front wheels. The bike should have a strong white headlight, a bell or horn, and a reflector. An orange safety flag mounted on the bike, which makes it more visible to cars, is also not a bad idea.

Like an automobile, a bicycle has to be frequently checked for flaws. The child himself should make it a regular habit to check his equipment, especially the brakes, each time before he rides the bike. He should also take the bike into the shop for a thorough overhaul at least once a year.

The Rules of the Road

In most cycling traffic injuries and fatalities, the cyclist is at fault. Often the problem is the bicycle rider's notion that he is not subject to the same laws as other vehicles. But he is! A bicycle *is* a vehicle. Many of the rules of the road that apply to cars apply to bicycles as well. To emphasize the seriousness of bike safety, you should always tell your child that the bicycle is a road vehicle, just as a car is. It can hit and hurt people and pets and it can get hit by other vehicles, which, except for other bicycles, will substantially outweigh it.

All of this means that the child has another set of "do's" and "don'ts" to add to his safety repertoire while riding a bike. You can make it easier for him to accept these new rules by linking them to the enjoyment he will have if he follows them. For an adolescent, you might also make them slightly more palatable by stressing how they prefigure the kinds of things he will have to be aware of when he steps up to what is probably his ultimate dream: driving a car.

Like an automobile driver, a cyclist must stop for red lights. He should not be riding on the sidewalk any more than a truck should. Older people and young children are especially endangered by reckless cyclists who are riding where they shouldn't be. Also like drivers, the cyclist must signal for a turn. Bicycles must ride on the right, going with the flow of traffic, just like cars.

Stay Alert!

Some localities are now prohibiting drivers from listening to walkaround-type portable stereos while operating a vehicle, and that should apply to the bike rider as well, who must be able to hear the beep of a horn. However, a cyclist should use his eyes as well as his ears to alert him to the approach of another vehicle, whose sound may be masked by the din of surrounding traffic.

Kids on bikes also have to be alert to many things that may not be of concern to drivers. For example, a cyclist can be endangered by his own pants! Pants legs should be held against the rider's legs by a clip or rubber band so they will not get caught in the gear and chain mechanism. He should also be wearing a safety helmet if he's going to be riding in traffic. Actually, it's a good idea for him to wear it anytime he rides. He should *avoid* heavy traffic, if at all possible. Talk to him about how traffic puts a crimp in the pleasure of riding. It's much more pleasant to go a few blocks out of the way to ride down a quiet, tree-lined street.

Hazardous Conduct

Unlike a driver, a cyclist should make left turns *on foot*. It's too dangerous for him to cut across traffic lanes when cars will not be looking for him. He also has to avoid slippery

surfaces, such as gravel. Storm drains and temporary surfaces containing slots and gaps which have been installed
for road construction are also special dangers for the
cyclist. If he's riding in traffic with friends, the only way to
do it is in single file. Since he will be riding close to parked
cars, he must be constantly alert for people suddenly
emerging from them.

Show-off behavior and general recklessness, which can
cause accidents anytime, are all the worse on a bicycle.
Remind him of the chant revered among child cyclists:
"Look, Ma, no hands. Look, Ma, no head." That also goes
for activities such as trying to carry a package in his hand
while steering the bike with the other. Packages belong on
a special rack or in a basket, and both hands belong on the
handlebars. Those handlebars, incidentally, were not made
for passengers, which he should carry only if he has a
special seat for them on the bike.

Although bikes come with lights to equip them for
night riding, and reflective clothing makes riders more visible, bike riding after dark is really an activity to be avoided
if it's not absolutely necessary. That's also true for riding in
inclement weather, when drivers are more caught up in
controlling their own vehicles and less attentive to the
cyclist who is harder to see and probably having even
more trouble controlling his bike.

A cyclist should *never* try to grab onto a moving
vehicle in hopes of getting a "free" ride. The dues that may
have to be paid for that ride are simply too high.

7

THE CHILD OUTDOORS

PLAY

Play. The very word evokes pleasure. Playing is a great way for a child to get healthy exercise and learn about the world and the other people in it—through symbolically acting out situations and feelings on a safe and controlled level. You can keep play positive and safe by taking some basic precautions.

Give two little ones shovels in a sandbox, and a difference of opinion may end up being settled with those shovels at close quarters. But if one of the children has learned to share instead of hit—there will probably be no conflict. Your own child's behavior will usually determine whether he has a good time or an accident.

The Playground

For many children, the local playground is the center for outdoor play. It should be—and usually is—a very happy place. To keep it happy, check your playground's equipment carefully and regularly.

All playground equipment should be firmly *anchored*. The mechanism that allows a seesaw to pivot on its bar should be *enclosed* to prevent little fingers from getting in. Climbing apparatus should be mounted over a *rubberized or other soft surface*. Slide rails should be a minimum of *2½ inches high*. Areas containing equipment such as swings should be *fenced off*, and *brightly colored markings* on the ground around them should indicate *danger zones*.

Playground Safety

If you have doubts about the safety of your local playground and would like to know what you can do about it, or if you're thinking of buying playground equipment of your own and want to know which safety features to look for, write to either:

U.S. Consumer Product Safety Commission
Washington, DC 20207

or

School and College Department of the National Safety Council
444 N. Michigan Avenue
Chicago, IL 60611

Most accidents are caused by the misuse of equipment. Swings and slides can be dangerous—even when the apparatus is designed to be as safe as it can be—if a child doesn't know how to use it safely. Here are some tips for safe playground fun:

- *Slides*. Parents tend to focus on getting the kids to wait for the previous user to clear the bottom of the slide before they begin their run. But most accidents on slides come from falls from the *ladder*—when kids slip in their

haste to get to the top or in their efforts to show off.
Keep an eye on your child *before* he comes down!

- *Swings.* Tell your child there can be only one person,
  sitting down, to each swing. He must walk at least five
  feet away from the swing, front or back. And the swing
  shouldn't go so high that he actually comes off it!

- *Seesaws.* Both partners must get off *together.* If parents
  are helping the children, one parent must hold the seated
  child while the other helps his partner off.

- *Monkey bars.* They're strictly off limits when wet. And
  they're for *climbing,* not jumping.

Playing Safely

As she expands her play terrain, a child will have to main-
tain a careful balance between her desire for adventure and
discovery and the need to adhere to the safety require-
ments you have been teaching her. The best way you can
help her is to give her some general principles of safety to
guide her in her games. For example:

- Don't play near traffic.

- Don't play in dangerous areas, such as building excavations or empty lots.

- Use equipment as it was intended to be used—for example, throw the ball, not the bat!

- Use proper equipment—such as a helmet for playing
  football and lights when bike riding at dusk.

Parents can help keep sports safe by working for safe
places to play in the community, organizing leagues to
provide a structured setting for sports, and encouraging

their kids to play in institutional sports programs run by schools, neighborhood organizations, churches, and synagogues.

You can also help your child gain a thorough understanding of the possible dangers of a sport by showing him the precautions taken by the pros. For instance, explain to the baseball initiate the reasons for a major league catcher's protective equipment. Then, relate it to the game he is about to play.

HOT-WEATHER SPORTS

When the sun is high and kids are out playing despite the temperature—be alert to the possibility of heat-related illness. This can range from a little light-headedness to heat stroke, a life-threatening emergency.

The first precaution to take is not to play at all outdoors when the weather conditions are extreme. There is no particular cut-off point; it depends on the sport, how the child feels, and where and how long it's to be played. Common sense dictates, for example, that it could be dangerous to play full-court basketball if it's ninety-five degrees outside with high humidity.

Dehydration

Kids who engage in athletics need to drink liquids frequently to prevent dehydration. Years ago it was thought that drinking water or juice while exercising would bring on cramps. But we now know that that is not the case. If your child has any doubts, ask him to watch a marathon race on television and note how often the runners reach out for cups of water during the event.

Symptoms of dehydration are:

- Dry lips and mouth

- Dizziness and nausea

- Confusion and cramps

For a mild case of dehydration, just let the child rest in the shade and sip water slowly. He will also need some salt. Don't give him salt tablets. They can disrupt the ratio of salt to fluids in the body. A more appropriate way of consuming salt is through a snack—even junk food, such as potato chips!

Heat Exhaustion

In more extreme cases of overexertion in the heat, exhaustion and stroke may result. If a child has heat exhaustion, you will probably see cramps and other symptoms of dehydration, as well as vomiting and a slight fever. Treat as you would a mild case and cool by fanning and the application of a cool compress.

Heat stroke is more of the same, with the possible addition of high fever and convulsions, a rapid pulse, and the cessation of perspiration. Treat the victim for heat exhaustion while you get someone to call the doctor immediately. While you are waiting for medical help, remove the child's clothing, massage his body toward the heart, and give CPR if you are trained in it.

Swimming

One of the best and most enjoyable antidotes to the heat is a plunge in a pool or ocean. Swimming safety rules consist of a few highlights of common sense! Tell your child to:

- Wait an hour after a meal before swimming.

- Make sure there's an experienced older swimmer around —preferably a lifeguard.

- Stay out of the water in threatening weather—and leave the water at the first sign of a storm.

- Be responsible. She should swim only where she feels fully at ease and dive only where a professional lifeguard says it's safe.

- Respect the water. No horsing around in deep water— ever. If this rule is disobeyed, the swimmer comes out of the water, fast.

If your child wants to swim away from shore, she must know how to swim strongly and well. She should also be able to float and tread water. If she gets in trouble, floating or treading water are invaluable for resting and staying in place until help arrives.

Teach her what to do if she gets a cramp in her leg. She can ease it by bending forward and massaging it with her hands, then straightening and flexing it once the pain has ebbed. This not only makes the cramp disappear; it also wards off the panic that causes most drownings.

What about lifesaving? Whether you or your (older) child is doing it, the old advice on the order of techniques still holds: *throw, row, go.*

1. Throw. A person who is (or thinks he is) drowning is likely to be in a panic. If you swim out to him, he may grab onto you so hard he pulls both of you down. So, your first attempt should be to extend an object—a pole, a piece of clothing, even your hand—which he can grab and by which you can pull him in.

96

2. Row. If he's too far out to reach with an object, get to him in a boat. Try to save him from the boat, rather than jumping in.

3. Go. If there's no way to throw or row, you'll have to swim out to him. But be ready to deal with the panic and the extra strength created by the flow of adrenaline. Tell him to be calm, for both of your sakes—and *keep* telling him. Explain that his calmness will save you both.

Once you have pulled him to safety, you may have to restore his breathing through mouth-to-mouth artificial respiration, which we discussed under First Aid. If he has no pulse, someone trained in CPR should get to work on him.

Boating
Boating is another great water sport—if you follow the rules:

- *All* children should wear life jackets, even if they know how to swim.

- No one should stand up in a moving boat. Instead, move slowly, hunched over.

- Stay with the boat if it capsizes. It won't sink completely, and it's a support to hang on to as you paddle to shore.

Horseback Riding
Back on land, we come to horseback riding.

Horseback riding only looks easy in the movies! Any child is small in relation to any horse, even a pony.

If the child stands in back of the animal he can get kicked, if he mistreats the horse he can get thrown, and if he is not careful he can simply fall off. Contrary to what the child may have thought, the horn on a Western saddle offers less protection than a security blanket. Horses may not be the brightest of animals, but they often have minds of their own. The child may think he's signaling the horse to walk to the right, while the horse thinks he ought to canter to the left.

There's only one rule for horseback riding: Children must take lessons and must always be under close supervision when they ride.

Hunting

Hunting is a dubious "sport." Its dangers are obvious and very lethal. For one thing, many children have unrealistic notions about guns that come from watching violent action television shows and cartoons. They may not fully grasp the finality of being shot dead. However, it's a tradition in many parts of the country to take children hunting, and if they are going to go, they had better learn the elements of safety at an early age.

Young, unsupervised children shouldn't hunt under any circumstances. They should be thoroughly familiar with the use and misuse of their weapon before they ever get to touch it—and then they should have to prove to their parents' satisfaction, while the gun is unloaded, that they know how to handle it. Supervised target practice should follow before they go out for the real thing. Once in the field, it should be made clear to them that they are expected to follow standard hunting safety procedures to the letter.

Fishing

Fishing is a much less threatening activity, except for the danger posed by the hook. Special care must be taken when casting, because anyone within the close vicinity of the fisherman is in potential jeopardy. Since children may go fishing without adult supervision, they should know how to remove a hook from their skin should an accident occur. If the barb has not entered the wound, simply slide the hook out. If it's gone in past the barb, and a doctor is not around, it must be pushed through so that the barb emerges (this is not applicable if the hook is in an eye, in which case a doctor must be summoned). Cut off the part containing the tip and the barb and then gently slip it out the way it got in. Let the blood cleanse the wound, then bandage it.

Walking and Hiking

Walking is a marvelous activity that provides interest and exercise throughout every stage of life. Even extended hikes over rugged country needn't be dangerous at all, if you approach them sensibly.

First, be sure you have:

- Proper clothing for both the anticipated weather and the terrain

- Sufficient food and water

- A first-aid kit

- A map

- A compass

- A noisemaker for each person to attract attention in case he gets lost

Next, consider the kids. No child should ever hike alone, and the younger ones should always be within sight and reach of an adult. Since accidents are most likely to befall tired children, the adult should call a halt when the junior member of the group begins to flag.

Getting lost in the woods can be a disastrous experience for anyone, and especially threatening to a preadolescent. Not that young children can't muddle through if forced to in an extreme situation. On July 2, 1983, an eight-year-old boy strayed from his family's camping expedition on Roan Mountain in Tennessee. A week later he was discovered near the peak, about 6,000 feet above sea level, alive and well. He had survived by eating wild apples and berries.

Most parents can do without such drama. And most kids, unless they've been raised in a rural area, wouldn't be able to tell poisonous from nonpoisonous berries. Since getting lost is always a possibility, albeit a remote one, you should discuss the possibility calmly with a child before setting off. He should be told that if lost, he should:

- Try to leave a trail. Carrying something with which to do that is a good idea—brightly colored plastic strips, for example.

- Climb to a higher point, so as to see where he is (if he can do it safely). If possible, he should look for some landmark by which he can orient himself.

- Follow a body of water downstream, where inhabited areas are usually found.

- If none of the above are helpful or apply, he should stay where he is and make a lot of noise. If he can, he should also build a smoky fire.

Country walks often mean meetings with country dogs. Such encounters are not always a joy to either party! Prepare for them by:

- Discussing the possibility with your child before you go out. Explain that the dogs out here are just the same as those in the city, so there's no need to be wildly afraid. The only difference is that farm dogs run to you from a distance, making it seem as if they're going to attack.

- Being calm yourself if you do meet a dog. Stand still with your arms by your sides. Let the dog sniff you and look you over. If you can, talk quietly to it. Then, holding your child's hand, slowly walk away.

In the rare case when the dog does bite, the wound must be washed free of saliva and bandaged. Then you must locate the animal's owner and inform him that it may have to be kept under observation to be sure it does not have rabies. Then get the child right to a doctor: Tetanus as well as rabies is a possibility.

Encounters with snakes may be minimized if you avoid the kind of countryside where they are found. Wherever you are walking, steer clear of rock piles with nooks and crannies. Be especially careful not to climb on such rocks where you have to put your hands into those holes in order to scramble up the rocks.

If you are walking in an area that is a habitat for poisonous snakes, read something about them in advance so that you can recognize one if you see it. The most dangerous snakes are:

- The pit vipers (*cottonmouth, copperhead,* and *rattle-snake*), which have fangs and small pits between their noses and their elliptical eyes

- The *coral snake,* identified by its brightly colored red, yellow, and black bands

The main treatment for a coral snake bite is to get the victim to a doctor as soon as possible. For pit vipers, there is some dispute as to what should be done. The standard treatment is:

1. Position the bitten part of the body below the heart.

2. Put a tourniquet above the wound (but not so tight that your index finger can't slip between the tourniquet and the skin of the victim).

3. Make an incision with a knife lengthwise over the fang marks.

4. Suck the venom from the wound for up to an hour with either a suction cup from a snakebite kit or your mouth. (Snake venom is not poisonous if swallowed in small quantities, although it could get into your bloodstream if you have a sore in your mouth.)

However, some say this method can interfere with circulation and produce an infection. It's important to realize that most people bitten by poisonous snakes do not die. Even if the venom was allowed to run its course, it would probably take at least twelve hours to kill. Since strenuous activity speeds the absorption of the poison by the body, the victim should be transported to help, if possible, or help should be brought to him.

Camping Out

Camping out can be a great experience for a child. Make it a safe one by being sure she knows how to handle any implements, such as a knife or hatchet, that she might use. Also reiterate precautions that must be taken with fire, which is at least as dangerous in the woods as in the kitchen. She should do nothing close to the campfire more active than toasting marshmallows or cooking under your watchful eye, and she should be careful not to stand close when she tosses wood onto the campfire, which will cause sparks to shoot off. Anything done in conjunction with the fire should be under your direct supervision.

WINTER SPORTS

Ice Skating

There's nothing quite like skating on a frozen pond. It's freeing, magical, wonderful. But, as you know, it can also be dangerous. Don't risk sending your child onto the ice unless it has been tested and the thin areas cordoned off. Even then—test it yourself, to be doubly sure.

Before your child goes out to play or skate on the ice, tell him what to do just in case he should fall through:

- *Don't* try to scramble back onto the ice. You'll probably fall right back into the frigid water.

- Instead, kick your feet behind you, as if you were going to swim.

- Then, maintaining a prone position to minimize the weight on the ice at any one spot, spread your arms wide and slowly pull yourself up onto the ice.

- Keep doing this, even if the ice keeps giving way. You'll move gradually toward the shore.

Skiing

From ponds to mountains—and skis. Of course skiing can be hazardous, but the chance of getting hurt is greatly minimized by skiing with safety in mind. Give your child these safety tips:

- Start with lessons and easy trails.
- On the trails, be aware of the other skiers—good and bad—around you.
- Never stop in the middle of a trail; pull off to the side.
- When your muscles tell you you've had enough, stop for the day.

If your child takes to the sport, get him his own equipment. Knowing what your equipment can do, as opposed to using somebody else's, is like being accustomed to a particular manual typewriter and then borrowing another one—try it some time. With your own ski equipment, you know how far you can lean when making a turn. The length of the pole will be the same each time, so your grip on it can become second nature. Your child can get a head start on safety by keeping that equipment in good shape.

Snowmobiling

Snowmobiling is fun, but the rider has far less control of the vehicle than a skier has over his skis. The machines weigh up to half a ton and go fast enough to create havoc in an accident. The rider is in the open and so is extremely vulnerable. If your child is going to use one, make sure she knows it's *not* a big toy. Unless you have absolute confidence in her maturity and ability to manage the vehicle, *you* ride with her.

If you let her go, make sure she:

- Is in the company of an older, responsible person
- Stays well away from highways and railroad rights-of-way
- Keeps to maintained trails

- Avoids frozen water completely

- Wears a helmet and goggles and carries a first-aid and repair kit

Frostbite

One serious problem to watch out for in all winter sports is frostbite. Skiers and snowmobilers have to take special care, since speed combined with cold produce a wind-chill factor that will do damage quicker than low temperature alone. At 0 degrees Fahrenheit with a 10 mile-per-hour wind, for example, the wind-chill factor makes the effect equivalent to −24 degrees Fahrenheit.

Unless you know what to look for, you may get frostbite and not be aware of it. How do you recognize frostbite?

- It begins with a reddening of the skin and a stinging feeling.

- Then the skin turns white—and has no feeling at all.

Because frostbite is hard to recognize in its initial stages, a child should always be with an adult if she's playing outside in very cold weather. She may not see the problem developing, but the adult will.

How do you treat frostbite?

- Do *not* rub it—not with ice, not with *anything*.

- Warm the affected area in clothing until you can reach shelter.

- Use warm water—*not* hot water or any other source of high heat—to raise the temperature of the skin until pinkness and feeling return.

- Check with a doctor.

8
AWAY FROM HOME

American children are some of the most well-traveled young people on this planet. Travel can and should be a positive, exciting part of their education. You can make it so by anticipating novel conditions they'll encounter and preparing them to meet them safely.

IN THE COUNTRY

For some urban kids, the country is like a foreign country. All of their young life they have been eating apples that came out of supermarket fruit bins. Now, suddenly, they are in a place where people eat them right off the tree! The local customs probably seem very colorful. But, as in true foreign countries, different ways of doing things can present some safety problems to the uninitiated. Here are some guidelines for undisturbed fun in the country:

- Don't eat anything off a bush until you've asked your host if it's safe.

- If you go out at night, even for a short distance, take a flashlight. Dark is *really* dark in the country.

- When walking on a country road, stay close to the side and face the oncoming traffic.

- Never hitchhike. Period. (Once you're in a car, it's not so easy to get out if you think you've made a mistake.)

- Enjoy animals from a safe distance. Uncle Sid's bull is not friendly old Ferdinand. Small, cute, furry things sometimes have rabies and almost always bite.

- Unless a knowledgeable adult is teaching you about it, don't climb on farm machinery, even when it's not in use.

SLEEPAWAY CAMP

Many urban and suburban kids get their first experience of the country at camp. School-age children going away to camp for the first time will have a happy and safe summer if they've developed safety consciousness in their daily lives. While a parent will, of course, want to discuss safe behavior with the child before she goes away, her basic education in avoiding and coping with safety hazards should have already been well under way by that time.

Your first concern is to choose a good, safe camp for her. Start by checking with the American Camping Association for information about camps that interest you. Write to them at:

American Camping Association
Bradford Woods
Martinsville, IN 46151

The camp you choose should have:

- An experienced, highly qualified director whom you like
- Counselors with documented experience
- A high rate of return of both campers and counselors
- Good health and emergency facilities
- A full-time nurse and an available doctor nearby

The summer before, drive up to the camp and drop in without warning while it's in session. Does someone challenge your presence on the grounds? Do the physical layout of the camp and its equipment present any hazards, especially waterfront or poolside areas and campers' bunks? Do you have an uneasy feeling about anyone there? If so, choose another camp.

THE BIG CITY

He's wide-eyed and a little overwhelmed. Almost everything he looks at is the biggest or most of its kind he's ever seen. He's a country kid in the city and he can't wait to explore. But his parents or hosts will not be doing him a favor if they fail to temper that enthusiasm with some necessary street smarts. Tell your child to:

- *Be alert to traffic.* In all the excitement, while he is constantly looking around and up, a child may not be watching where he is going. Tell him to be on the alert for turning cars, trucks, and buses and for trucks backing up in commercial districts.

- *Stay out of crushes on the sidewalk.* Rush hours bring hordes of people to the sidewalks just outside office buildings. And they *are* likely to be rushing—and capable of knocking down a small child. Preschoolers should hold an adult's hand at all times. Older children should be told to avoid the middle of crowds that might gather to watch a street performance or any other spectacles that collect large numbers of people in a small area in a metropolis. Aside from the possibility of being trampled if something happened to make the crowd move suddenly, a child may be victimized by pickpockets and other types of rip-off artists.

- *Have his name, vacation address, and phone number on him always.* If he gets separated from the adult who was accompanying him, he should go straight to the store manager or a policeman.

- *Carry a map.* Older kids going out on their own should remember that cities look quite different on foot from the way they appeared through a car window. Even if you've driven through the streets, you can get lost in them as a pedestrian. A map will help both the child and anyone who tries to help him find out where he is and where he wants to go.

UNFAMILIAR WEATHER
A child traveling far from home may encounter weather she has only heard about. Some of it may be pretty extreme. Although you don't want to frighten the child, prudence suggests she become familiar with any type of adverse weather condition peculiar to the place she's

110

visiting.

If she's traveling to the Midwest or South, she should know something about hurricanes and tornadoes. Tell her:

- Tornadoes tend to occur in the late afternoon of a spring or summer day.

- If there's a hurricane or tornado warning, get away from the shore (where there may be surging waves, floods, and winds of over seventy-five miles an hour).

- Try to go below ground (a basement in a house, or a ditch or shelter outside).

- If there's no basement in the building, the center of the structure is the safest place. Once there, take shelter under something solid.

- Mobile homes are *absolutely unsafe* in a hurricane or tornado.

A trip to other parts of the country, particularly certain areas of California, means a slight risk of experiencing an earthquake. Since there is no such thing as an earthquake warning, other than the long-term predictions Californians always live with, the only thing one can do is react on the spot. It will help to know that:

- The safest place is a completely open area, away from buildings and electric wires.

- If caught inside, the best spot is under something sturdy, such as a table.

After the quake passes, the main danger is from fire started by broken gas lines and collapsing structures—so it's a good idea to stay at home for a while.

FOREIGN TRAVEL

Children—especially younger children—should be prepared for a foreign trip well in advance. Reassure them that
people are the same all over the world: Everyone likes kids.
Your child should know that if he ever gets lost, someone
will be willing to help him, even if he can't speak their
language. Show him the identification tag you are making
for him. On it, in the language of the country to which you
are going, should be his name and the address and phone
number of the hotel or home where you are staying.
Instruct the child to point to it if he gets lost.

Spend as much time as possible before the trip talking
about the country to which you will be going, with special
emphasis on crucial ways its customs differ from what he's
used to. For example, tell him:

• If they drive on the other side of the road

• If the tap water is unsafe to drink

• What the traffic symbols mean

• How to recognize a policeman

Assuming he does not know the language, familiarity
with a few simple words and phrases will make him feel
more secure. If he's old enough, make a game out of learning them. "I am lost" is a good one to start with. (Even if
they speak English at your destination, there may be misun-
derstandings. The "subway" in London, for example, refers
to a passage underneath a street. The "underground" is the
equivalent to our subway.)

CHILDREN TRAVELING ALONE

When is a child capable of traveling alone? Consider the
temperament of the child. If she seems secure enough, and
can be relied upon to read signs and follow directions, then
she may be ready. However, you should check in advance
with the company that will transport her. Trailways will
only permit independent travel for kids eleven and older;
on Amtrak, she has to be at least twelve. If the child
changes her mind and panics as the trip approaches, call it
off. If you don't, she is likely to be nervous and accident-
prone.

If she's going by bus, introduce her to the driver and
make it clear that he's the first person to go to for assistance. Airline flight attendants are usually great with kids.
Talk to them about your child, even though the airline will
notify them to expect her on board. Although you will see
the child off and friends or relatives will greet her at the
other end, make sure she knows how to make a collect call
and remind her that if there is any problem in a terminal,
she should seek help from uniformed personnel.

If your child is going overseas alone you must make all
the necessary arrangements well in advance and persis-
tently check with the airline to make sure they haven't
slipped up in any way.

When Lila and Dudley sent Anna, their eleven-year-old
daughter, to Germany to visit her grandmother, they did
just that. The airline provided a chaperone who met Anna
at the check-in counter and escorted her to her seat on the
plane. She was seated near the kitchen, where the stewards
and stewardesses could keep an eye on her, and she was
given a little holder for her ticket and passport that she
could hang around her neck. In Munich, another chap-

113

erone delivered her to her waiting grandmother, who had to "sign for her" (the child is handed over *only* to the person specified). The chaperone also stayed with her as she went through customs and got her luggage, in order to expedite the process. And there was no extra charge for this extra service.

9

MUGGINGS, ABDUCTION AND SEXUAL ABUSE

Parents may feel a good deal of anxiety in discussing this subject with their children—especially the sexual aspect, because of the kind of violation it involves. But here, perhaps more than in any other area of child safety, it's important for parents to approach the threat and the child's response in a calm and rational way. As Sally Cooper of the Child Assault Prevention Project in Columbus, Ohio, recently wrote: "By talking to children in nongraphic, nonviolent language about potential dangers and how to safely maneuver in their world, we replace their fear with confidence, strategies, and real information."

At some point, you will have to start giving your child the run of her neighborhood. One way to effect a transition between supervision and complete independence is to have the child follow a schedule or specific route known to you if, for example, she is beginning to walk home from school by herself. The condition of this arrangement would be that she report any deviation from the plan by phone.

When discussing with a child the dangers in her increasingly expanding world, and when setting rules and limits to cope with those dangers, parents should explain their fears specifically. Tell your child of your anxieties. She may not completely accept your reasoning, but she will probably empathize with your feelings. Similarly, respect her fears and encourage her to talk about them.

Monitor your child's reaction to your discussion. Some children have unrealistic notions of how much power they have in some situations, even if it involves being attacked by several older children. Overconfidence is no more helpful than wild and unreasonable fears. Confront the child with reality and explain why fear can sometimes be useful in helping us evaluate and not exacerbate a dangerous situation.

AVOID "BAD" AREAS

One of the most painful aspects of preparing a child to be safe in the streets is dealing with the concept of "bad" areas. It is painful because, in fact, we are usually referring to neighborhods that are characterized by their racial, ethnic, or economic makeup. There are many urban and suburban areas in which it is not safe for a black child to walk through an all-white neighborhood, and vice versa. We owe it to our children to be candid about these facts, but also about why such things are so, in order not to replace fear with hatred.

HOW TO AVOID BEING A VICTIM

Once the child has a sense of the relative danger of certain areas and situations, you can give him the practical information he needs to avoid being a victim of street crime. Tell him:

- *Walk erect, briskly, and purposefully, with eyes looking steadily forward.* Your walk and attitude can be strong defenses. You won't look like an "easy mark" if you appear to know what you're doing and where you're going.

- *Don't make eye contact with anyone who looks suspicious.* Some people take such contact as an invasion or a sign of hostility. It also calls attention to yourself—which you don't want to do.

- *Sit by the driver on a bus or train. If that's not possible, sit near the door.*

- *Stay awake and alert on all public transportation.* Daydreaming is a very creative activity, but a bus or subway is a bad place for it. Your body language is an important defense when you're sitting down, too. Also, you need to keep your wits firmly about you to make sure anything you're carrying is secure.

There are some standard safety rules for walking on the street and entering a building which a child should learn as early as possible—certainly before she is out on her own:

- *Stick to the beaten path.* Being surrounded by people doesn't guarantee safety, but it increases your chances of avoiding harm. Short cuts are dangerous—precisely because they're less used. Alleys and other dark and narrow areas should always be avoided.

- *Don't look worth robbing.* Carrying personal stereos and wearing expensive watches and clothing where you might be at risk is asking for trouble. The same goes for

flashing money if you should have an occasion to open
your wallet.

- *Take advantage of the people on and just off the street
who may be regarded as informal watchmen* (not to
mention the protection offered by the policeman on the
beat, if there is one). Examples are doormen, merchants
with sidewalk displays, and shopkeepers who tend to be
near the front window, such as shoemakers. There may
be a "Safe Haven" or other such program where you
live, in which storekeepers and homeowners identify
themselves as places of sanctuary for a child in trouble. If
so, make sure your child is familiar with their symbol
and knows where at least some of them are on her
route.

- *Remember that the safest place to walk is in the middle
of the sidewalk, not along the curb or building line.*

- *Do not get into an elevator with someone who makes
you feel uncomfortable.* You can snap your fingers,
mutter about how you forgot something, and walk out.
You can wait for the elevator to return if it's headed for
the basement. If you're on the elevator with someone
who makes you anxious, push a button for the next
floor and get off before he realizes what's happening.
Always note the location of the alarm button.

- *If you sense you are about to be accosted in the street,
try to walk into a store or toward other people.* If you
can't do that, try looking past the potential attackers to
an imaginary group of people in the distance, call out to
"them", and then rapidly move in that direction. If

somebody menaces you while you're near other people, scream without embarrassment as loud as possible. If nobody responds, scream "fire" to force people to get involved. (Make sure your child understands the difference between this and giving a false alarm.)

- *If, despite all these precautions, you are accosted on the street, swallow the humiliation, cooperate, and give up the money or possession.* Arguing or shows of bravado are definitely out. They may enrage the mugger and provoke physical attack. Because of the "macho" element in our culture, boys may need extra support on this point. Teach them that the most important thing anyone can do in a robbery is to remain calm.

IN CASE OF ATTACK

Some parents send their kids to martial arts classes, anticipating a mugging and hoping that their son or daughter will be able to deal physically with a mugger. That may work, but it may also get the child killed. A better bet might be the ancient art of Aikido.

Terry Dobson, an Aikido expert, stresses the calming influence of this technique as a more relevant skill in a crisis than the more purely physical martial arts, such as Karate. Briefly, Aikido does not emphasize particular holds or maneuvers but rather the reduction of emotional turbulence so that the individual may think more clearly. The concept of "centering" is vital to Aikido. Imagine a point about two inches below your navel. Focus on it and project all your negative feelings into that spot. Let your muscles relax, straighten up, and breathe deeply. This is practiced until it comes naturally.

If the child is physically attacked, either by surprise or in spite of her sensible actions, tell her to take a fall and stay down until the assailant has gone.

If he seems hell bent on seriously hurting her, she can try passively falling back as he lunges at her, turning, and taking advantage of his momentum, spinning him around and then running for her life. Other than that, her only recourse is to hurt him by fighting as dirty as she can. Fingernails, teeth, and any sharp objects within reach are all legitimate weapons at that point, and any area of his body is fair game.

ABDUCTION

Children have to know how to regard strangers. But young children often have trouble understanding exactly what the word *stranger* means. And you don't want to load the concept with menace and raise a fearful, antisocial child.

The angle to stress is not the fact that the person is unknown to the child. Rather, discuss that person's behavior combined with the fact that the child does not know him. One child psychologist has suggested that your tone in discussing the subject should be no different from the one you might use in "telling your child to finish his vegetables."

Your child should not be frightened because someone she doesn't know says something to her. There are, after all, many adults who like children and may spontaneously speak to them with the best of motives. More important is what they say, and what they might ask a child to do.

The stress should be on seeing how the child might interpret a stranger's actions and words, and her progress in learning how to discriminate between the innocuous and the inimical. If your child is old enough to understand the idea of being careful of "Greeks bearing gifts," tell her the story of the Trojan horse.

This is an excellent time for "What if..." questions. The content should focus on all the situations you can conjure up in which an adult might try to entice a kid to come with him. You could start off with, "What if someone you didn't know offered you candy to get in a car with him?" and make them increasingly more subtle as the child assimilates the ideas and information. You could build up to, "What if someone who seemed to know me said I had sent him to pick you up at school?"

You will have to go slowly with the child until about the age of eight. So keep it simple and don't be upset if he garbles it or gets it all wrong. Just patiently go over the same material again.

Tell your child that if she's approached by a stranger who wants her to go with him, she must say no and walk the other way. If he's persistent and follows her, she can always hint that her parent is waiting for her just around the corner. Similarly, if she's alone in the house and someone she doesn't know phones and asks if her parents are home, she can make up a story about one of them being in the shower. And *you* can help her by not putting her name on her lunchbox and other items, which would make it possible for a stranger to address her by name and thus gain instant credibility.

Fingerprinting
One controversial way that some parents have been dealing with the possibility of their child being kidnapped is to have her fingerprinted so that she may more easily be traced. But, as an official of the American Civil Liberties

Union pointed out recently: "There is a serious potential for invasions of individual privacy. The fingerprints could be misused at some point and involve children in criminal investigations." Some programs allow the parents to keep the prints in their possession, but that may create a practical problem. They may misplace them or keep them somewhere—a bank vault, for example—where they would not have constant access to them.

What to Do If a Child Is Missing

If you're out shopping and discover that your child is missing, stay calm. Look behind counters, and through doorways such as those leading to dressing rooms and near colorful displays that might attract a child. If you still can't find him, go immediately to the store guard, or to the manager. Then check in other nearby stores or movie theatres. (Of course, your child should be instructed to go to the nearest security guard should he become separated from you while out shopping.)

If you "lose" your child around the house, look in the basement, car, and behind any open door in a neighbor's house. Check behind man-made objects and behind bushes and trees. Don't forget closets, either, or under beds and other furniture. He may have gone to a friend's or neighbor's house, trailed after older kids, or even be hiding from you.

If none of this pans out, then call the police.

SEXUAL ABUSE

Notwithstanding our obsession with strangers, sexual abuse is more likely to be found at home, or close to it. The assailant usually turns out to be a family member, neighbor, or someone else who knows the child.

Teach Your Child to Say "No"

We can protect our children from sexual abuse by building up their ability to say "no" and enlarging their concept of their rights with respect to their bodies. Force is usually *not* an element in the sexual abuse of children. Knowledge and understanding are children's best defense.

They must learn the concept of *limits*. There are some things to which they don't have to accede, especially if demanded by adults. These include touching or looking at the child's sexual parts and the adult asking or insisting that the child do the same for him. Here you literally need to "put words in their mouth," since they need an anatomical vocabulary to discuss the subject. (If you find yourself putting that off, examine your own attitudes which might be blocking you from having that discussion. Your child's safety is far more important than your delicacy.) Make sure your children understand the concept of "privacy," and why sexual areas are referred to as "private parts."

When discussing this with a child, it's important to keep a matter-of-fact tone, with no panic or excessive emotion. You may want to explain to your daughter that, at some point later in life, she will want to engage in activity involving such touching with someone she cares about. But when that happens, it will be of her own volition.

Part of the supportive atmosphere in which children can absorb this lesson comes from the freedom they have (or should have) to reject lesser displays of unwanted affection. They should not *have* to be kissed and hugged by demonstrative friends and relatives, for example, if they don't want to be. If someone insists on doing that even when told clearly not to, children should be free to tell them bluntly just how they feel. The politeness and automatic respect most children are taught to show adults

123

simply because they're older can actually become a destructive response for a child upon whom an adult later tries to push more intimate contact.

The "Why's" of Child Sexual Abuse
Children are likely to want to know why an adult would sexually exploit them, and will probably not accept characterizations of such people as monsters. In many cases, the person in question may be someone the child retains affection for, while at the same time being confused and upset by their invasive and strange behavior.

It makes more sense, and it is closer to the truth (which children appreciate), to speak of child sexual abusers as lonely to the point of being disturbed, unable to make relationships with older people, or with so many problems that they don't know what they are doing. Characterize the person as someone who needs help. A child can empathize with that. Most children are occasionally lonely or have trouble forming relationships with their peers.

A Conspiracy of Silence
In order for this kind of illicit relationship to go on for any length of time, there has to be a *conspiracy of silence* between the adult and the child. A very young child could be enticed, at least initially, with the idea of playing an extraordinary game that will remain their secret. The adult may purchase the child's silence with a threat: humiliating him by threatening to tell "what he did," divulging some other secret, or even threatening to harm someone close to the child, or his pet. But more likely there is some kind of bribe involved. It may be material, but the medium of exchange could actually be a kind of affection.

Often the exploiter plays on a child's lack of affection

124

at home, offering the child a "special" relationship. To him, that child is very special, and their relationship is special. The child may accept this *if his home life does not provide him with the affection he so desperately needs.*

It is important for the child to understand that a promise of secrecy about something which he or she now realizes is harmful *need not be kept.* In fact, a best-selling children's book has been written on this subject, Oralee Wachter's *No More Secrets For Me* (Little, Brown).

How to Detect Child Abuse

If there's a conspiracy of silence, how can you know that something is going on? Be alert to all your child's signals, all the time. Things may be revealed indirectly through behavior, such as a sudden and dramatic increase in sexual sophistication. The child's sudden and unexplained aversion toward an adult could be another warning signal.

How to Deal with Child Abuse

What should you do if you discover such a relationship? First of all, make sure you know what you've uncovered. Two children of approximately the same age engaging in sexual exploration is a natural part of growing up. But if your child is being sexually exploited, you will have to decide how you will deal with the adult involved. That may not be an easy decision: a court case could mean your child will have to testify, an experience that could be traumatic. Or the person implicated may be someone close to you. One possible solution is to get that person to agree to get help, and to stay away from your child.

But more important than what happens to the adult is how the child feels about what has happened. And there the responsiblity falls on you. You must make it clear to your son or daughter that it was not their fault. Your child's perception of what it all means will come from you. Dr. Suzanne Sgroi of the St. Joseph College Institute for the Treatment and Control of Child Sexual Abuse in West Hartford, Connecticut, has said: "The sexually abused child may not feel abused initially, but as the child learns what society thinks of what he has done, the child feels betrayed. He feels he cannot trust adults or family members. The child has a sense of danger, a sense of being violated, a sense that he is not as good as he was before."

The child who has been sexually abused should be encouraged to talk about it whenever and however he or she desires. Long-term effects vary with the child, the length and extent of the abuse, and the relationship to the adult involved. Psychotherapy may help a great deal.

The ultimate solution for child abuse is something that society as a whole will have to produce. Dr. Benjamin Spock may have said it best when he recently wrote:

> My basic wish is that we all work to make our society much less violent, much less aggressive, much less competitive. I believe that all neglected and abused children should be rescued early through much better and more extensive social services. All schools should be kindly. I believe that children should not be punished physically. In this kind of world, where every child would be raised with respect and love, there would be a dramatic reduction in the number of kids who grow up to be kidnappers, murderers or child molesters...

Most of all, show your children that you love them and understand their pain. Love works healing miracles.

APPENDIX

QUICK REFERENCE FIRST AID

Shock

Symptoms: Perspiration, cool and pale skin, weak but rapid pulse, distant look in eyes, possible vomiting.

Treatment: Calm the child and keep her warm, elevate her feet, moisten lips, get doctor.

Bleeding

Treatment: For serious bleeding, victim should lie down and injured part of body be raised unless fracture is suspected; apply pressure over wound, put new bandage over old if bleeding continues, apply pressure to pressure points, use tourniquet only if nothing else works, get help.

Fractures

Symptoms: Pain, misshapen limb, swelling, bluish discoloration, extreme tenderness.

Treatment: Support and immobilize affected area with splint, bandage, or sling; do not push on open fracture; try not to move child if fracture to head, neck, or back is suspected; get doctor.

Burns

Symptoms: First degree—pain and redness; second degree—blisters and sores; third degree—skin turns black or white and tissue under it is exposed, damaged nerves may numb pain.

Treatment: First degree—soothe under cold water and clean; second degree—soothe with cold water, apply cold compresses, bandage (don't break blisters), and go to doctor; third degree—don't remove any clothing stuck to burn, pour cool water on it, elevate affected part of body, bandage if possible, get medical help immediately.

Electric Shock

Treatment: Remove child from source of current without endangering yourself, give mouth-to-mouth breathing assistance if breathing has stopped and CPR (if you have training) to restore circulation, check for burns.

Poison

Treatment: Have child drink water, call poison control center, induce vomiting with syrup of ipecac if appropriate.

Choking

Treatment: Immediately perform Heimlich Maneuver.

Eye Injury

Treatment: Do not rub, flush out corrosive substance, only doctor should remove object stuck in the eye.

Ear Injury

Treatment: Only by doctor.

Overexposure to Heat

Symptoms: Dry lips, nausea, dizziness, confusion, cramps; vomiting and fever in more extreme cases; convulsions, rapid pulse, and cessation of perspiration in heat stroke.
Treatment: Water and salty food for mild cases; fanning and cool compress if more extreme; removal of clothing, massage, and CPR for heat stroke, as well as immediate medical attention.

Drowning

Treatment: Mouth-to-mouth breathing and CPR.

Overexposure to Cold (Frostbite)

Symptoms: Skin turns from red to white and stinging sensation is numbed.

Treatment: Don't rub, keep warm, use warm water to restore normal skin condition, have it checked by a doctor.

Poison Snake Bite

Treatment: If coral snake, transport victim to doctor; if pit viper, use tourniquet, incision, and suction (some dispute over this), and transport victim to doctor.

POISON CONTROL CENTERS

Consult your local telephone directory for the poison control center nearest you. If there isn't one in your area, try one of the following regional centers (since numbers change, it would be a good idea for you to confirm in advance the number of the center you would call in an emergency):

California 800-662-9886

Georgia 800-282-5846

Iowa 800-362-2327

Idaho 800-632-9490

Maine 800-442-6305

Michigan 800-572-5396

Nebraska 800-642-9999

New Hampshire 800-562-8236

Ohio 800-762-0727

South Dakota 800-592-1889

Utah 800-662-4225

Washington 800-572-5842

Wyoming 800-422-2704

Colorado, Iowa, Kansas, Missouri,
South Dakota, Wyoming 800-228-9515

National Center for the Prevention and Treatment of Child
   Abuse & Neglect
1204 Oneida Street
Denver, CO 80220
303-321-3963

Department of Special Education
California State Unversity
5151 University Drive
Los Angeles, CA 90032
213-224-3283

Child Abuse and Neglect Resource Center
Suite 208
157 Yesler Way
Seattle, WA 98104
206-624-1062

CHILD ABUSE INFORMATION

If you have reason to suspect a child is being abused, call
the Child Abuse and Maltreatment Reporting Center at
800-342-3720.

For further information on child abuse, contact the
Child Abuse and Neglect Resource Center nearest you
(these are regional federal government centers):

Judge Baker Guidance Center
295 Longwood Avenue
Boston, MA 02115
617-323-8390

College of Human Ecology
Cornell University, NVR Hall
Ithaca, NY 14853
607-256-7794

Institute for Urban Affairs and Research
Howard University
P.O. Box 191
Washington, DC 20059
202-686-6770

Regional Institute for Social Welfare Research
P.O. Box 152
Athens, GA 30601
404-542-7614

Graduate School of Social Work
University of Wisconsin, Milwaukee
Milwaukee, WI 53201
414-963-4184

Graduate School of Social Work
University of Texas at Austin
Austin, TX 78712
512-471-4067

Institute of Child Behavior and Development
University of Iowa, Oakdale
Oakdale, IA 52319
319-353-4825

CHILD CARE AGENCIES AND ORGANIZATIONS

The following national and international organizations are valuable sources of information and assistance regarding day care. To learn what they have to offer, write:

American Home Economics Education Association, Inc.
2010 Massachusetts Avenue, N.W.
Washington, DC 20036

American Parent's Committee, Inc.
1346 Connecticut Avenue, N.W.
Washington, DC 20036

American Red Cross
Director, Nursing and Health Services
17th and D Streets, N.W.
Washington, DC 20006

Association for Childhood Education International, Inc.
3615 Wisconsin Avenue, N.W.
Washington, DC 20016

Child Development Associate Consortium, Inc.
805 Fifteenth Street, N.W.
Washington, DC 20005

Children's Defense Fund, Inc.
1520 New Hampshire Avenue, N.W.
Washington, DC 20036

Coalition for Children and Youth, Inc.
815 Fifteenth Street, N.W.
Washington, DC 20005

Day Care and Child Development Council of America, Inc.
805 Fifteenth Street, N.W.
Washington, DC 20005

Family Impact Seminar
1001 Connecticut Avenue, N.W., Suite 732
Washington DC 20036

National Association for Child Development and Education,
   Inc.
1800 M Street, N.W.
Washington, DC 20036

National Association for the Education of Young Children,
   Inc.
1834 Connecticut Avenue, N.W.
Washington, DC 20009

National Committee for Citizens in Education
410 Wilde Lake Village Green
Columbia, MD 21044

National Committee on Household Employment, Inc.
7705 Georgia Avenue, N.W.
Washington, DC 20012

National Council of State Committees for Children and
    Youth
1614 Garfield
Laramie, WY 82070

National Organization for Women
Task Force on Child Care
45 Newberry Street
Boston, MA 02116

National Parents Federation for Day Care and Child
    Development, Inc.
429 Lewis Street
Somerset, NJ 08893

The Non-Sexist Child Development Project
Women's Action Alliance
370 Lexington Avenue
New York, NY 10017

Organization Mondiale Pour Education Prescolaire
    (O.M.E.P. World Organization for Early Childhood)
1319 Denby Road
Baltimore, MD 21204
(sponsors International Year of the Child)

EMERGENCY PHONE NUMBERS
911 or Other General Emergency Number _____

Family Physician
Name_____
Address _____
Telephone _____

Local Hospitals
Hospital Name_____
Address _____
General Telephone _____
Emergency Room Telephone_____

Hospital Name_____
Address _____
General Telephone _____
Emergency Room Telephone_____

Nearest Police Precinct
Precinct Number _____
Address _____
Telephone _____

Poison Control Center
Location_____
Telephone _____

Parents at Work
Mother's office _____
Address _____
Telephone _____

Father's office _____
Address _____
Telephone _____

Schools

Child's Name _____
School _____
Address _____
Telephone _____

Child's Name _____
School _____
Address _____
Telephone _____

Parent's Authorized Representative for Medical Emergencies

Name _____
Address _____
Home Telephone _____
Work Telephone _____

Neighbors

Name _____
Address _____
Telephone _____

Name _____
Address _____
Telephone _____

Name _____
Address _____
Telephone _____

Name _____
Address _____
Telephone _____

Relatives

Name_____
Address _____
Home Telephone _____
Work Telephone _____

Name_____
Address _____
Home Telephone _____
Work Telephone _____

Name_____
Address _____
Home Telephone _____
Work Telephone _____

Children's Friends

Name_____
Address _____
Telephone _____

Name_____
Address _____
Telephone _____

Name_____
Address _____
Telephone _____

Name_____
Address _____
Telephone _____